HERE'S
TO THE
MEN
OF
ALTON

HERE'S
TO THE
MEN
OF
ALTON

STORIES OF COURAGE AND
SACRIFICE IN THE GREAT WAR

TONY CROSS

The
History
Press

First published 2015

The History Press
The Mill, Brimscombe Port
Stroud, Gloucestershire, GL5 2QG
www.thehistorypress.co.uk

British Library Cataloguing in Publication Data.
A catalogue record for this book is available from the British Library.

ISBN 978 0 7509 6077 9

Typesetting and origination by The History Press
Printed in Malta by Melita Press

Front cover: H Company, 2nd/4th Hampshire Regiment in India in 1915,
including men from Alton (author's collection)
Frontispiece: The Cross of Sacrifice, Alton (author's collection)

'Dulce et decorum est pro patria mori'
'It is sweet and fitting to die for your country'

Horace (65BC–8BC)

Men of Alton

Here's to the men of Alton!
Who gave their lives to gain,
Fresh honours for their Country
And the old flag to retain.
Then forward, men of Alton!
The vacancies to fill
Of those who fell
And fought so well,
For honours they have gained.
It's all for righteous causes
That we are in the fray
To crush the Huns,
Destroy their guns,
And make the Kaiser pay.

Pte H. Gilliam
RAMC with the BEF
Hampshire Herald & Alton Gazette, 16 January 1915

CONTENTS

FOREWORD

My interest in the men of Alton who lost their lives in both world wars began in the autumn of 2000 when I was asked to talk to a local Cub Scout group, in which my son was a member, before they paraded at the Remembrance Day commemoration. I had previously written an article on the town's war memorial but realised I knew little about the men whose names were recorded on it.

The local community bore witness to the sacrifice of many of their young men during both major conflicts of the twentieth century. However, with the passing of the years, an awareness of this sacrifice has gradually been lost. As curator of Alton's Curtis Museum, itself part of the war memorial, I felt it was a task I should undertake to ensure that the men who had died were not forgotten. Appeals in the local press resulted in contact with resident families who had lost relatives and much relevant material came to light. Over time, more details were discovered and those about whom nothing was known were gradually reduced. Following my departure from the museum in 2011, I continued this research so that their sacrifice would be recognised by the local community a century later.

Numerous people have contributed a considerable amount of work and time in following the hundreds of leads from a wide variety of sources and I give my thanks for their valuable assistance, particularly to Jane Hurst. I am also grateful to Ruth Boyes at The History Press for her editorial input. Any errors contained here are entirely my own.

The result is a collection of information relating to those young men who were lost in the Great War, including in which unit they served, where and when they died, and where they are buried or remembered. Visits to the battlefields are nothing new; indeed they began while the war was still being fought. However, I would like to think that today's Altonians taking Continental holidays might locate cemeteries, mainly in Belgium and France, that contain the last resting place of those local men who went off to fight for King and Country fully expecting to return to the pleasant market town that, a century later, we are also pleased to call home.

Tony Cross
2015

LIST OF ILLUSTRATIONS

Sources of Illustrations

Author: 3, 5, 7–10, 19, 21, 27, 29, 30, 32–34, 36, 43, 46, 47, 53, 55, 58–60, 65, 66, 69, 72–74, 76, 80–82

Commonwealth War Graves Commission: 56

Hampshire Cultural Trust: 6, 11, 12, 16, 18, 22–26, 40, 44, 45, 51, 61, 68, 75, 77–79

Royal Naval Museum: 4, 14, 17, 28, 37–39, 41, 49

Royal Hampshire Regiment Museum: 2

Forces Postal History Society: 9

Private collections: 1, 13, 15, 20, 31, 35, 42, 48, 50, 52, 54, 57, 62–64, 67, 70, 71

INTRODUCTION

On Sunday, 28 June 1914, the Austro-Hungarian Archduke Franz Ferdinand and his wife Countess Sophie were shot and killed in Sarajevo, the capital of Bosnia-Herzegovina, then part of the Austro-Hungarian Empire. It was their fourteenth wedding anniversary.

The Austro-Hungarian Government believed that the Serbian Government had been involved in the assassination, so Austria-Hungary declared war on Serbia exactly one month later. Serbia's ally, Russia, began preparing for war against Austro-Hungary. Austria-Hungary's ally, Germany, declared war on the Russian Empire on 1 August 1914, and Russia's ally, France, declared war on the German Empire on 3 August 1914. The German Army was ready to invade France by marching through Belgium, announcing their intention of doing so with or without Belgian permission.

Until now the British Empire had not paid much attention to these events. However, in 1839, several countries, including Great Britain and Prussia (as Germany was then called), had signed a treaty promising to respect the independence of Belgium. The British Government therefore threatened war with Germany, unless the German Army retreated from Belgium. When they failed to comply with this demand, the British Empire declared war on Germany on Tuesday, 4 August 1914.

Hampshire was one of the first English counties to see military activity. The Royal Navy base at Portsmouth had become one of the greatest dockyards in the world. Meanwhile, the British Army had been concentrated at Aldershot, ready to defend the South Coast of England or travel by railway to Southampton, from where they could be carried by troopships for service throughout the British Empire. At Farnborough, the Royal Engineers began experimenting with observation balloons and man-carrying kites – activities that led to the formation of the Royal Flying Corps and the Royal Aircraft Factory.

The presence of much of the British Army, Navy and Air Force in Hampshire, meant that those forces were best placed to help on mainland Europe. The British Expeditionary Force (BEF) moved by road and rail to Southampton and landed in France on Friday, 7 August 1914.

CHAPTER ONE

1914

———————— THE BUILD-UP TO WAR ————————

On Saturday, 4 July 1914, the death of Archduke Ferdinand the previous Sunday was not headline news in the *Hampshire Herald & Alton Gazette* (*HH&AG*). Being a local newspaper, there were local stories – including the visit of the Lord Mayor of London to the Treloar Cripples Hospital. However, a national item was also featured – the death of Joseph Chamberlain, the politician father of Neville Chamberlain who took Britain into the Second World War twenty-five years later.

Next to an advertisement for local ironmonger T.M. Kingdon & Sons, towards the bottom of page 6, was a small piece headed 'Austrian Heir Assassinated – a double attempted tragedy'. Three short paragraphs outlined the event followed by a section on the new heir presumptive, Archduke Charles Francis Joseph, the eldest son of the murdered prince's brother, who had died in 1906.

Subsequent editions of the newspaper carried no further information about the diplomatic storm and it was not until 25 July that Altonians had any real idea of the unfolding drama. The report of a visit by King George V to Spithead for a weekend with the fleet, mentioned that the event 'had been curtailed by the delay caused by the political crisis which prevented him arriving until Saturday evening'.

Larger reports related to the North East Hampshire Agricultural Society, the Overton Sheep Fair, the funeral of 69-year-old Montague Knight of Chawton House and the marriage in New Zealand of Godfrey Burrell, a member of the well-known Alton brewery family. It was also reported that the 48-mile-long (77km) Panama Canal would be opened to traffic on 15 August.

The edition of 1 August 1914 reported the death of printer Mr C.J. Moody, who lived on Normandy Street, and included details of the Horticultural Society Flower Show held in All Saints' vicarage meadow. It was not until page 5 that the developing war was mentioned. An international news report mentioned mobilisations of many countries, including Russia:

Austria and Serbia at War – Capture of Belgrade – Russia's Mobilisation – Martial Law in Germany – Grave situation throughout Europe.

Austria-Hungary declared war on Serbia on Tuesday afternoon. Germany has declined to accept Sir Edward Grey's conference proposal. Negotiations between Austria-Hungary and Russia were reportedly broken off on Wednesday, but an exchange of telegrams took place between the German and Russian Emperors. It was reported on good authority on Thursday that Germany had presented to Russia what amounted to an ultimatum, asking for an explanation of the partial mobilisation ordered by the Government and requesting an early reply.

Sir Edward Grey [Foreign Secretary] told the House of Commons on Thursday that he was unable to say the European situation was less grave than on the previous day. He added that Great Britain was continuing to pursue the one great object of preserving European peace, and for that purpose was keeping in touch with the other Powers.

1. 1914–15 embroidered silk card.

2.   RMS *Caledonia* transported the 2nd/4th Hampshire Regiment to India in late 1914.

This article ended with a note, 'The Oak of Peace at Jena, Prussia which was planted in 1816 in commemoration of the downfall of Napoleon, was by a strange coincidence struck by lightning and burnt to the ground almost at the moment of the reception at Belgrade of the Austrian declaration of war.'

The following week, 8 August, page 3 of the newspaper led with 'The Great War of 1914' and printed regular reports for the next four and a half years.

──────── LOCAL MEN IN THE HAMPSHIRE REGIMENT ────────

On Saturday, 25 July 1914, men from Alton in the 4th Battalion (Territorial Force) travelled in two trains to Bulford on Salisbury Plain for annual training, although mobilisation had yet to become a driving force. On 4 August, the battalion marched to Salisbury and took a train to Portsmouth where they camped at Hilsea. When their place in the defences of Portsmouth was taken by the Special Reserve Battalion, the Territorials returned to Bulford Camp.

Within a few days of the outbreak of war, members of the Territorial Force, which had been raised for home service only, were asked to volunteer for action overseas. Invasion did not seem particularly likely so these units were not needed at home. Whilst they were not considered ready to reinforce the BEF, they were up to the task of relieving Regular units overseas to enable them to support the Regular Army.

The 4th (Foreign Service) Battalion, now the 1st/4th Battalion, left Bulford on 9 October 1914. Thirty-one officers and 800 men reached Southampton and embarked on HMTS *Ultonia*, described as 'a pretty old Cunarder of about 10,000 tons', where they were joined by the 6th Battalion, bringing the total number of men up to 1,600.

Along with five Union Castle liners, a P&O vessel, a British India Steam Navigation ship and an escort of two Royal Navy cruisers, they set sail for India, passing Cape Trafalgar on 14 October, Malta on 18 October and Port Said on 22 October before spending three days at Suez. They docked in Bombay on 9 November, where they travelled by train north to Poona (now in northern Pakistan), arriving on 11 November and settling into Wanowri Barracks.

The 1st/4th Battalion left Poona for Rawalpindi, some 1,600 miles (2,500km) away, on 9 January 1915 and on 7 March they were mobilised for action. On 13 March, they left Karachi on HT *Elephanta* for Basra in the Persian Gulf, arriving four days later.

800M 8/14 H W V Forms
B. 218c.
1

Army Form B. 218c.

NOTICE.

MEN ARE REQUIRED for all branches of the Regular Army,

and, if medically fit, will be accepted on the following conditions :—

1. FOR THE DURATION OF THE WAR :

Height, 5 feet 3 inches and upwards.
Chest, at least 34 inches.
Age, if ex-regular soldiers, 19–42 years ; other men, 19–30 years.
Married men or widowers with children will be accepted and will draw separation allowance under Army conditions.

2. FOR THE FOLLOWING PERIODS according to the Arm which they join :

CAVALRY, INFANTRY, and ARMY SERVICE CORPS, 7 years with the colours, 5 years in the Reserve.

ROYAL HORSE and ROYAL FIELD ARTILLERY, ROYAL ENGINEERS, 6 years with the Colours, and 6 years in the Reserve.

Height, 5 feet 3 inches and upwards.
Chest, at least 34 inches.
Age, 18–25. Married men are not accepted.

Men wishing to join should apply at any Military Barrack or at any Recruiting Office ; the addresses of the latter can be obtained from Post Offices or Labour Exchanges.

GOD SAVE THE KING.

3. Recruiting handbill, 1914.

The 2nd/4th Battalion, formed in September 1914, had thirty officers and 756 other ranks, including H Company, which was composed of Alton men. With the 4th Devonshire Regiment and the Duke of Cornwall's Light Infantry, they sailed for India on 12 December 1914 on HT *Caledonia*. Calling at Port Said, Bombay, they disembarked at Karachi after a voyage of a month and two days. They then boarded a train for Quetta (now in Pakistan) some 800km to the north. An account of this journey appeared in the *Regimental Journal* of March 1915, and ends with, 'Thus we came to Quetta in the time of the Great War of 1914–15'.

They were not there for long before they were on the move again, leaving Karachi on 29 April 1915 in HT *Chenals* for Suez. Upon their arrival on 15 May, they started to prepare for action and received instruction following on from their 'life-like frontier training', undertaken in India. The men then moved to Gaza in Palestine where they were involved in the fighting that began in November.

——— BELGIAN REFUGEES – A PERSONAL STORY ———

The De Jonghe family from Mechelen, north of Brussels, were forced to leave their home in August 1914 as the Germans overran Belgium. With many other families, they travelled north to Antwerp. Here they were forced to flee into neutral Holland where they were sent to Amsterdam by train and put in a camp that was:

> … surrounded by a high fence of barbed wire and guarded day and night. My granny, aunt and uncle and their baby who were with us, accepted an invitation to go to England as they feared for the life of their child through ill health in the camp. My father couldn't find a job in Holland and because more and more children were becoming ill, he decided that, rather than returning to our home which was now occupied by the enemy, to try to take us to England.

In Rotterdam, they took a steamer to Tilbury and then journeyed to London by train. Earl's Court had been turned into a reception centre for refugees and they stayed there for three weeks whilst their relatives, who had been placed in Alton, sought permission from the Alton Belgian Refugee Committee for the family to join them. On arrival in Alton they were greeted at the station by the Belgians already here and walked to the Pavement, formerly Conduits Hotel, a building on the High Street currently occupied by TSB.

> We had a nice bedroom on the first floor overlooking the street so that we could see what was happening outside. We went very easily to bed that night but couldn't get to sleep owing to a band playing and people singing, preaching and praying in the street below.

The next day they discovered that the noise had came from the Salvation Army, who were holding their usual Saturday evening meeting. There were six Belgian families in the building, although a few weeks later two of them left Alton; one to France, the other to London to work, and two more families replaced them.

> The Pavement was a big house with many rooms and a big garden with the River Wey running swiftly through it. There were two small wooden bridges across the river to go to the vegetable gardens near Vicarage Hill. The garden was an ideal playground for the children to run about in with their friends and there was even a way out to Market Street. One or two garden parties were held in the garden on behalf of the Belgian Refugee Committee.

Some of the Belgians worked in the sawmills, one in the brewery in Turk Street, whilst Mr De Jonghe worked in the gardens at Morland Hall for Mr Ferrand, as well as for the Lowis family of Amery House. The children were unable to go to school as the schoolrooms were occupied by Scottish soldiers. When the troops left Alton in 1915, however, the schools reopened and the three De Jonghe children (Lodewyk the eldest, his younger brother, René and sister, Melanie) were sent to the National School, now St Lawrence Primary School. When the eldest left he was recommended for Eggar's Grammar School but the family, who had lost everything, could not afford the fees. Lodewyk was instead apprenticed at the printing works of Edwin Moody, No. 62 Normandy Street, between the cinema and what is now the fish and chip shop.

4.   William Robinson and George Ray were lost when
     HMS *Aboukir* was sunk on 22 September 1914.

As they found employment, the Belgian families left the Pavement one by one until only two remained and, by 1916, the building was closed. One family went to live in Ashdell Road, in a cottage belonging to Mr Ferrand near the old paper mill, whilst the De Jonghes went to Lenten House, home of the Burrell family. After a spell working in the printing trade in London (a continuation of his pre-war occupation), Mr De Jonghe came back to Alton and did gardening around the town before getting a job at the Thornycroft factory in Basingstoke. With the closing of the Basingstoke–Alton railway he walked home and back to Basingstoke every weekend, lodging near his work during the week. When Lenten House was sold in 1918 the family moved to Basingstoke where Lodewyk also managed to get a job in the factory.

Interestingly, Lodewyk, who kept in touch with many Altonians, wrote in 1972 that:

> Basingstoke was a bigger town but we preferred Alton, because we knew quite a lot of people and we considered ourselves as Altonians. We were very sorry to leave Alton and I'm still very grateful to all the Altonians who helped us in one way or another during our exile in this pretty and peaceful small Hampshire town.

The family returned to Belgium in the spring of 1919 '… to find Mechelen had changed a great deal; everything seemed so poor and miserable, there were a lot of damaged houses with most of the furnishings removed, but nevertheless, we enjoyed peace again'.

Apart from a few reports in the local newspaper, today there is no trace of the presence of Belgians in Alton during the Great War.

THREE BEFORE BREAKFAST

During the early months of the war the Royal Navy kept a patrol known as Cruiser Force C, in the southern North Sea. Many thought they were vulnerable to attack by the German Navy and the patrol was nicknamed 'the live bait squadron', but the Admiralty maintained the ships on the grounds that destroyers were not able to operate in the frequent bad weather.

Early on the morning of 22 September 1914, three rather old cruisers – HMS *Cressy*, HMS *Aboukir* and HMS *Hogue* – were sighted off the Dutch coast by the German submarine, *U9*. They were going slower than the regulation speed of 11/12 knots and travelling in a straight line rather than zigzagging to avoid detection.

At 6.25 a.m., *U9* fired a torpedo at *Aboukir* which hit on the port side. She took on water, lost power and the order to abandon ship was made as she started to sink. As it was thought she had hit a mine, the other two vessels came to pick up

5. The jubilant return of German U-boat *U9* to Wilhelmshaven following the sinking of three British cruisers, 23 September 1914.

survivors, but on their arrival, two torpedoes hit *Hogue* and her engine room began to flood. They were clearly under attack and *Cressy*, spotting a periscope, set off for safety. The *U9* still held three torpedoes; two hit *Cressy* on the starboard side and then a final, decisive blow caused her to sink within fifteen minutes. Nearby merchant ships picked up 837 men from the three devastated cruisers but 1,459 perished, many of them reservists or cadets. Two Royal Marines from Alton, Sergeant George Ray and Corporal William Robinson, were amongst those lost on *Aboukir*.

Following the attack, major ships were ordered to travel at a rate of 13 knots, zigzag throughout their journey and refrain from stopping in dangerous waters. The commander and crew of *U9* were given a hero's welcome on their return to their base at Wilhelmshaven the following day and they were awarded the Iron Cross for the action.

Pause for Thought

Late in 2011 it was reported that salvage was taking place on the wrecks of HMS *Hogue*, *Cressy* and *Aboukir* and representations were made to the Dutch Ambassador. It later transpired that the British Government had sold the wrecks to a German salvage company in 1954 and all protection that they would have had as war graves was lost. Today, these salvage rights have been bought by companies who have begun taking apart the British ships as their iron, steel and copper are now so valuable.

6.   Alton Abbey Gatehouse.

ALTON ABBEY

The Order of Saint Paul (OSP) was a Church of England religious community founded on the work of Revd Charles Hopkins in 1884 and first practiced by merchant sailors in the river ports of India and Burma.

Recognising the need for a British base for recruitment, training and fund-raising, Hopkins founded a house at Barry Docks, near Cardiff, and a second foundation was established at Alton in 1895 to help care for out-of-work and aged sailors. A third community house opened in Greenwich in 1897 to serve the Port of London. The OSP regulated its life with an adaption of St Benedict's Rule, and the members made their vows of poverty, chastity and obedience.

The monastery at Beech near Alton was initially composed of tents and huts of wattle and daub, which were gradually replaced by corrugated-iron build-ings. The permanent accommodation on the site began with the building of a gatehouse with an attached chapel in 1901, followed by the establishment of the abbey church within a few years. Alton Abbey (as well as the Greenwich Priory) became involved in caring for German sailors serving on board British merchant ships at the outbreak of hostilities in August 1914, as Father Hopkins knew that the alternative for them would have been prison. The monks and their associates became the operating authority for what were at first described as 'concentra-tion camps', although Father Hopkins later moderated the description to that of 'Abbey Alien Seamen's Camp'. The first group arrived on 10 August and by the end of the month the figure had risen to about 200.

7.   'Sweeping the Germans off the Earth', a satirical postcard of 1914.

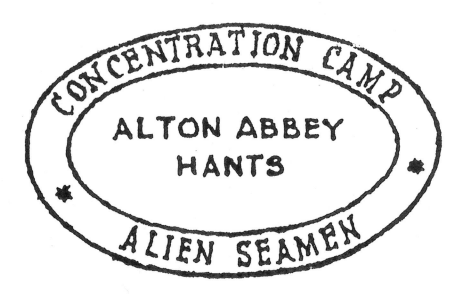

8.   A censor's mark used at the Camp for Alien Seamen at Alton Abbey in 1914.

ALTON, HANTS,

OCTOBER 24TH, 1914.

FELLOW TOWNSPEOPLE,

I find Martial Law prohibits public speaking on the action of the Authorities.

I promoted this Meeting, and intended to speak and move a resolution. I have no wish to break the law. A short time in our excellent local police quarters would not hurt me, but our object has been obtained without it. Our assembly is **a Protest** against the loose way the 200 or more " Germans " at Beech have been guarded.

At our Urban District Council Meeting. I said they might (no matter the characters given them **by their friends**) run amuck. They have done so, costing the Ratepayers many pounds to round them up. Armed guards with bayonets fixed had to give a great display, motor cars and police taken off their regular duties to catch the undesirables. Why ? Because only a few Boy Scouts made the guard. Is it fair to the boys or us ? **I say NO !**

I believe two more squads have since arrived, and these are vouched for as simple simons. After the butchery of our Soldiers, our Allies Women and Children, we still protest. **We want none of them.** What we only ask for them, is to be ringed in with barbed wire and a stout guard, we will then keep our powder dry.

"God Save The King."

G. FROST,

SUNNYSIDE, ALTON.

J. G. Clement, Printer, Alton.

9. An open letter from George Frost regarding the German seamen at Alton Abbey, 24 October 1914.

10. La Touret Memorial to the Missing, France.

Guarded initially by local Boy Scouts, who gained a 'War Service' badge for their efforts, there were a few 'domestic' disturbances that resulted in some prisoners being moved to a camp at Frith Hill. The continued lack of a military guard seems to have upset some locals and a public meeting was arranged. However, due to fears that the meeting would be an offence under the Defence of the Realm Act, it was cancelled and Councillor George Frost circulated a letter on the subject instead.

The residents were subject to Home Office rules, which were approved in October 1914, and were treated as if they were members of the abbey family. However, without prior warning some eighty men and boys were removed by the military on the orders of the War Office on 15 April 1915, marched to Medstead station and taken to an unspecified destination.

At the start of hostilities, each of the monks were released for war service. Four from Alton Abbey would never return, having, in the words of Father Hopkins, 'offered the Supreme Sacrifice'. They were Brother John English, and Associate Brothers James Grierson, George Hood and William Barnes.

Brothers Aidan and Mark remained in order to prevent the closure of both the abbey and the priory.

THE BEF IN FRENCH FLANDERS 1914–15

In October 1914, part of the BEF moved north from Picardy and took up positions in French Flanders where they were immediately engaged in the series of

11. A stereoscopic photograph showing part of the village of La Bassée, which was devastated after the fighting of October 1914 during the 'race to the sea'.

attacks and counter-attacks in an attempt to out-flank the enemy that became known as the 'race to the sea'.

Between 12–29 October 1914, the 2nd South Lancashire Regiment took part in the fighting at La Bassée. The attack resulted in terrible losses and on 21 October alone they lost seven officers and more than 200 men. Nevertheless, the line was never breached. Private A.E. Mason from Alton was a member of this unit. He was reported missing on 24 October 1914 but his death was not confirmed until March 1916.

THE BRITISH RED CROSS SOCIETY

The Voluntary Aid Detachment (VAD) was established in Alton in 1911, with Mrs Gott as vice president and her retired husband, Colonel George Gott, as honorary secretary. He was succeeded by Mr Guy F. Ferrand of Moreland Hall in 1914. Two detachments were formed: Hants 84 with Mrs Gott as commandant and Hants 198 under Mrs Lee.

The Red Cross Hospital in Alton, one of seventy established across Hampshire, opened on 30 October 1914 with fifty beds, later increased to eighty-four. Patients were received from the Cambridge and Connaught Hospital, Aldershot, and the medical officers were local doctors H.C. Williams, O.V. Payne, W.E. Bevan and E. Leslie. Volunteer nurses treated a total of 2,100 patients in Alton during the Great War. The average cost per patient per day rose from 2s 4½d (13p) in 1915 to 3s 3d (16p) in 1916, 3s 4d (16p) in 1917 and 3s 9½d (19p) in 1918.

Donations raised £1,086 11s 4d (£1,086.56), whilst the army grant, at the rate of 3s 3d (16p) per patient per day, was £10,616 10s 5d (£10,616.52). There were regular reports in the *HH&AG* relating to the generosity of the local community, giving garden produce, useful goods and services. An article in the summer of 1917 lists: silk, butter, eggs, fruit and vegetables, cakes, flowers, clothing, milk, garments and bed boards as well as money. On 31 December 1918, the hospital closed and Mrs Violet Gott of Will Hall was later awarded an MBE.

BELGIAN SOLDIERS ARRIVE

Alton people have had the terrible effects of war brought before them this week by the presence in their midst of 48 wounded Belgian soldiers, who arrived on Saturday afternoon last [31 October]. They are what are called 'convalescent cases', although all of them are only in the first stage of recuperation, and all are suffering from wounds, some bullet, some shrapnel and others wounds by the bayonet.

They are in the Red Cross Hospital in the Assembly Rooms and the patients are from the Royal Victoria Hospital in Folkestone and the Bevan Hospital in Sandgate. The youngest of the patients is a lad of 16, Charles Cueppen who joined the Belgian Army a month before the war.

On Saturday [31 October 1914] the Red Cross received about 50 wounded Belgian soldiers. Everything was in readiness. The Assembly Rooms have been converted into an excellent hospital, with every comfort and convenience. And the ladies are unremitting in their careful nursing by day and night. On Sunday the weather being fine, many of the wounded sat out in the Square, and attracted a large number of visitors, who gave them fruit, flowers, chocolates and cigarettes. Their presence continues to be a great attraction especially to the women, girls and children, and it is amusing to hear the efforts, on both sides, to make themselves understood. Several ladies and gentlemen of the neighbourhood take our foreign guests for motor rides. Under the very favourable conditions here the poor fellows are sure to improve rapidly.

HH&AG, 7 November 1914

12. Wounded Belgian soldiers arrive at the Red Cross Hospital in the Assembly Rooms, October 1914.

13. Embroidered silk card showing the flags of the Allies, including Italy, which entered the war in May 1915.

THE BATTLE OF CORONEL

On 1 November 1914, the Battle of Coronel took place off the coast of Chile. Vice-Admiral Graf Maximilian von Spee defeated Rear-Admiral Sir Christopher Cradock when a number of German ships – including the armoured cruisers *Gneisenau* and *Scharnhorst* – took on the Royal Navy squadron.

Cradock had orders to fight rather than flee, and stuck his ground even though the odds were against him. The resultant destruction of HMS *Good Hope* and HMS *Monmouth* was a victory for Spee, who lost just three men in the battle, although the German force also used half their ammunition, which was impossible to replace. The cost to the British side was far greater, however, and 1,600 officers and men were lost, with Cradock and Stoker L.R. Wright of Normandy Street, Alton, amongst them. Shock at the encounter resulted in the sending of more Royal Navy ships, which in turn destroyed Spee and the majority of his squadron at the Battle of the Falkland Islands the following month.

14. Lloyd White was lost when HMS *Good Hope* was sunk at the Battle of Coronel on 1 November 1914.

JOHN HARDING

John Harding of East Worldham who was serving in HMS *Viking* was very severely wounded in the action fought in the Bight of Heligoland, died on Monday [16 November] as the result of his injuries in Deal Hospital, where he was conveyed after the action. He was buried on Thursday [19 November] at Deal with full military honours. The deceased was only 24 years of age.

HH&AG, 28 November 1914

On 28 August 1914, the Battle of Heligoland Bight became the first naval engagement of the Great War. The British Fleet arrived off the north-west German coast, where much of the German Fleet remained in safe harbours. A number of long-distance sorties and scouting missions took place on both sides before the British sent a fleet of thirty-one destroyers with two cruisers and submarines to ambush the German destroyers. Four German ships were sunk and three were damaged, with 712 casualties, 530 injured and 336 taken prisoner. The British suffered four vessels damaged, thirty-five casualties and fifty-five wounded. On their return to Britain, the ships and their crew were met by cheering crowds to celebrate the victory. The lasting effect of the encounter was to restrict the freedom of the German Fleet for it was encouraged to remain in port and avoid any contact with superior forces.

15. Jack Harding, who served on HMS *Viking* (the only ship in the Royal Navy with six funnels), died on 16 November 1914 from wounds received at the Battle of Heligoland Bight.

A ROYAL VISIT

Yesterday [Friday, 20 November 1914] the three children of HM King Albert of Belgium visited the Red Cross Hospital at the Assembly Rooms where some 50 soldiers of the Belgian Army wounded in the war are being nursed by the Alton VAD [Voluntary Aid Detachment] of the British Red Cross Society. The visitors were HRH Prince Leopold, Duke of Brabant, aged 13, HRH Prince Charles, aged 11, and HRH Princess Marie, aged 8.

Alton gave them a fine reception. In the Hospital Square the children from Eggar's Grammar School and the elementary schools of the town formed up in double rows, while the Belgian refugees who are receiving hospitality in the town were given an honoured position inside the hospital. A crowd of fully 1,000 people waited patiently for the arrival of the Royal visitors. Shortly after 3 p.m. the Princes and Princess attended by the ladies and gentlemen in waiting, drew up at the top gate to the Square having motored over from Hackwood Park where they were the guests of Lord Curzon.

They were received with loud cheers and the schoolchildren eagerly waved their pocket-handkerchiefs. Alighting in the roadway the honoured visitors walked through the lines of cheering children round the Square to the hospital entrance where they were received by Mrs Gott, Commandant of the VAD, and staff. The depth and warmth of the reception seemed to surprise the Royal guests who walked shyly and smiling faintly at the assembled crowd.

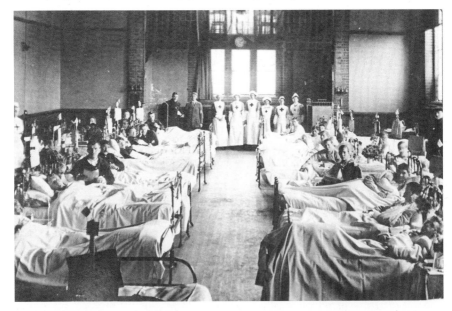

16. The main hall of the Assembly Rooms was Ward A of Alton Red Cross Hospital.

Inside the hospital they quickly lost a great deal of their shyness and shook hands with and talked freely to many of the wounded soldiers. Naturally this was a red-letter event for the Belgians in Alton. After spending about an hour at the hospital the Princes and Princess returned by motor car to Hackwood Park.

HH&AG, 21 November 1914

The logbook of the National School, now St Lawrence Primary School, recorded on Friday, 20 November 1914, that: 'Some of the children have been taken by an assistant teacher to see the Belgian Princes and Princess who are paying a visit to the Red Cross Hospital in the town.'

HMS *BULWARK*

HMS *Bulwark* was attached to the Channel Fleet, patrolling the English Channel. The vessel had been moored, loading ammunition for some days on the River Medway, almost opposite Sheerness, Isle of Sheppey, Kent. On Thursday, 26 November 1914, around 7.35 a.m., she exploded and, when the smoke cleared, the ship had vanished.

17. Three Alton men were amongst those lost when HMS *Bulwark* blew up on 26 November 1914.

From a crew of 750 just fourteen survived and two later died of injuries. During January 1915 many bodies of the *Bulwark's* crew were washed up on the Kent coast. Some were identified but many were not. Eighty-two unknown sailors are interred in Woodlands Cemetery, Gillingham, seventy of which were buried in a communal grave. Alton lost three men in this tragic accident – H.C. Arnold, H. Morgan and A.E. Webb.

The ship had been commanded by Captain Guy Sclater and his body was identified and returned to his home town of Odiham for burial, which took place on 2 December 1914. A family commemorative plaque can be found in All Saints' church, Odiham.

1914 PRINCESS MARY'S GIFT

Amongst the most well-known items that have survived from the Great War is a small yellow tin embossed with the portrait of a young woman, two 'M's, the names of our six allies and 'Christmas 1914'.

In a gesture reminiscent of her grandmother, Queen Victoria, who sent a tin of chocolate as a gift to troops fighting in the South African War at Christmas/New Year 1899/1900, Princess Mary launched something similar in October 1914. Her Christmas Gift Fund resulted in the production of the Princess Mary Gift Box.

Most of the troops received the tin gift box containing an ounce of pipe tobacco, twenty cigarettes, a pipe, a lighter, Christmas card and photograph. A tin for non-smokers contained a packet of acid tablets, a writing case containing pencil, paper and envelopes, as well as the Christmas card and photograph of the princess. The needs of minority groups were also considered and sweets and spices were substituted for the tobacco products in respect of gifts to Indian troops. Nurses received a tin containing chocolate and a Christmas card.

Problems with supply resulted in alternative items being included but some 426,724 gifts were distributed on Christmas Day. An indication of the special regard in which the box was held was that, whilst many enjoyed the contents, others sent their box home. In view of the large numbers of British, Colonial and Indian troops serving elsewhere (around 1.8 million men), their gift was sent in January and comprised the box, a New Year's card and a bullet pencil.

Other memorabilia from the war may include a brown-coloured tin that once contained chocolate. On the lid is: 'A gift of the Colonies of Trinidad, Grenada and St Lucia to His Majesty's Naval and Military Forces.'

On Sunday last, Alton was invaded by two Battalions of the Royal Scots Regiment. It is true that the invasion was not unexpected, being in fact a week overdue, but it was welcome – welcome in more ways than one. It was welcome to the inhabitants generally and the shopkeepers in particular, and after a week's experience of the men the general and unanimous verdict is that they are 'very nice laddies'. Both Battalions marched from Aldershot where they had been in Barracks, and at the end of the twelve-mile march they looked fresh and fit. They came in full war paint. The band of the Alton troop of the Boy Scouts marched out with colours flying to play them in, but the Regiment had brought their own pipe band. Crowds were in the streets to welcome them.

The 12th marched in first, punctually at 1 o'clock, and went straight through the town to the west end, where the Battalion split itself up into companies for the various districts. A quarter of an hour later came the 11th Battalion, and they took up their quarters in the east end of the town and Holybourne. So well was everything arranged that within an hour the men had been allocated both to their quarters in empty buildings and also in private houses.

The elementary schools hold by far the largest number of any buildings, one school being occupied by troops from each Battalion. Normandy House and the large stores behind found accommodation for nearly 300, while large

18. A group of the Seaforth
    Highlanders who were billeted in
    the town in early 1915, pictured
    on what is now part of the
    forecourt of Amery Hill School.

bodies are also quartered in the Drill Hall, the hop kiln behind Mr Kemp's Yard and in empty houses in various parts of the town. Both Battalions are up to full strength, so there are at least 2,300 men in the town. There is a fair sprinkling of veterans in the regiments, and most of the men have done 3 months training, some of course less than that, a few being recruits of a few weeks.

The following Monday was a windy, wet and miserable day and it was found that several of the outbuildings used as billets were unsatisfactory for the men and a risk to health, and a large number made a welcome change to billets in private houses on Tuesday.

HH&AG, December 1914

Households in the town were paid for housing and feeding soldiers. In 1964, C.W. Hawkins gave the Curtis Museum a copy of the army agreement signed by his mother during the Great War:

I am willing to billet the troops quartered upon me and provide subsistence in accordance with the Army Act, under particulars given below for the sum of two shillings and six pence per man per diem [day].

Particulars:

Lodgings and attendance.

Breakfast: Six ounces of bread, one pint of tea with milk and sugar, four ounces of bacon.

Dinner (hot): One pound of meat previous to being dressed, eight ounces of bread, eight ounces of potatoes or other vegetables, no beer or minerals, other food of equal value to be substituted.

Supper: Six ounces of bread, one pint of tea with milk and sugar, two ounces of cheese.

(Signed) J. Hawkins
Address: No. 23 Amery Street

A conversion of the units used above is as follows: 2s 6d is equivalent to 12.5p but in terms of value (using the retail prices index) it would be worth about £10.30 today. Pounds and ounces were the units of weight at that time, 1lb (consisting of 16oz) is equivalent to 454g, 1oz is 28.35g. The measure of volume at that time was the pint (and following only partial metrication it is still used in pubs today), which is equivalent to 0.568 of a litre.

NEW YEAR'S EVE

The year 1914 closed and the year 1915 was welcomed in a unique manner. Never had Alton witnessed a Scots New Year's Eve – Hogmanay. This important function was organised by the officers and men of the Royal Scots (11th & 12th Battalions), and about 1,600 of them assembled in the great cellar at Messrs Crowley & Co's brewery. The place was decorated with evergreens and flags, and an excellent four hours concert was arranged. The memory of those present was impressed by the sight of the khaki-clad men who sang the favourite chorus 'Tipperary'. Military and civilian friends and the Alton Band assisted with the programme. At midnight a fairy announced the New Year's wish 'Royal Scots. Good Luck!' Cheers, Auld Lang Syne and the National Anthem closed the gathering.

In the streets, as the soldiers dispersed, it was estimated that there were about 3,000 people (soldiers and civilians). Bagpipes were playing, and so dawned the stirring year of 1915.

HH&AG, 2 January 1915

CHAPTER TWO

1915

GOODBYE

It is with a very keen sense of regret that the Alton people part with the 11th & 12th Battalions of the Royal Scots, who move out from Alton today (Saturday), going back to Aldershot. During their six-week stay in the town, the men, by their conduct and character, have made themselves well and truly liked by everyone. It is no exaggeration to say that in many of the billets the men will be remembered for many a long day to come, and Alton people will watch their fortunes with interest when they go up to the front. A very real friendship has sprung up between the townspeople and the Regiment, and the good feelings expressed by the townspeople and the efforts made on all hands to make the stay of the regiment a pleasant and happy one has been cordially reciprocated by the officers, non-commissioned officers and men.

Their place is, we learn, being taken by battalions of the Black Watch and the Seaforth Highlanders, and we are sure the same hearty welcome will be extended to them and the same measure of goodwill and comradeship shown as has been shown to the regiment which is leaving.

HH&AG, 16 January 1915

PATRIOTIC FAMILIES

On 13 February 1915, the *HH&AG*, which was maintaining a Roll of Honour for local men who had enlisted, carried a small piece in its 'Alton War Notes' column that Mrs Newman of Blackmoor, who had five sons serving at the front and one in the navy, had received a letter of congratulation from the king. It seemed that Mrs Newman also had seven relatives serving in the armed forces.

The following week, the newspaper mentioned that they had been contacted by two more patriotic Alton families who also had multiple sons in the

19. A 1915 embroidered silk card depicting the flags of Britain and her Allies.

20. Patriotic families, those with multiple members in the services, were regularly featured in the local press early in the Great War. The sad, inevitable consequences as the war progressed, were multiple family deaths as casualty figures rose.

forces – Mr and Mrs Bowers of French's Court on the High Street, who had five sons in uniform (William, George, Archie, Edwin and Leonard) as well as a son-in-law who was also serving; and Charles Andrews who had three sons in the Hampshire Regiment and another in the Hampshire Carabineers.

This led to a regular feature, for two weeks later the following were mentioned – Mr and Mrs Coleman of Vicarage Hill, who had four sons in the army and navy, one of whom had since died in the navy (Alfred Coleman – ship's carpenter), and Mr and Mrs J. Hawkins of No. 71 Ackender Road, who had four sons in the forces (George – a chief yeoman of signals, Royal Navy; Stephen – a sergeant in the Army Service Corps; Charles – a sergeant in the 5th Battalion of the Queen's Regiment in India; and William, who was invalided from the Scots Guards).

LETTERS FROM INDIA

From Captain Godfrey Burrell:

> H (Alton) Co. 4th Hants. Rawalpindi, India

> … tell Alton that when they have done with the Royal Scots there are just a small band of men called H Company 4th Hampshire Regt on the Indian Frontier that want just a little notice from home.

Private B.F. Chesterfield sent a letter to Mr W.B. Trimmer (his former employer):

> … I notice by the *Hampshire Herald* that the Royal Scots billeted in Alton are having a jolly good time. Don't you think it is unfair to the Alton boys out here for strangers to come and take everything, to be treated like their own sons, when we are out here and entirely forgotten? The men from Ropley had a pipe and some tobacco sent to them for Christmas, and yet we had nothing, not even a line wishing us the compliments of the season. Would it be too much to ask if you could get some tobacco and cigarettes sent? We don't get much pay, it averages 5 chips or 6s 8d [roughly 33p] per week and it costs a jolly sight more to live out here.

> Hoping you and yours are in perfect health.
> Ben. F. Chesterfield

> *HH&AG*, 6 March 1915

The editor added a rather terse note:

Private Chesterfield scarcely does Alton people credit. A cablegram was sent from Alton to H Company at Christmas wishing them good luck and the compliments of the season. Mr W.B. Trimmer informs us that he will be pleased to receive gifts or money to buy tobacco and cigarettes for the Alton men in India.

21. H Company, 2nd/4th Hampshire Regiment in India in 1915, including men from Alton.

THE SEAFORTHS IN ALTON.

WHEN FIRST THE RUMOUR GENTLY SPREAD,
 OF OUR BILLETING DOWN HERE,
OUR HEARTS WERE FILLED WITH AWFUL DREAD,
 OF A VILLAGE BLEAK AND DREAR.

BUT HERE WE ARE, AND WANT TO STAY,
 SHALL I SAY, TILL PEACE IS MADE?
HOW SAD OUR HEARTS WHEN WE GO AWAY,
 IN SEARCH OF A NEW PARADE.

WILL, —"ABSENCE MAKES THE HEART GROW
 THE FEELINGS OF ALTON DISPLAY?   [FONDER,"
WILL, —"OUT OF SIGHT, OUT OF MIND"—ECLIPSE IT,
 WHEN THE SEAFORTHS GO AWAY?

22. Poem written in the autograph book of an Alton lad by Angus Livingstone, Seaforth Highlanders, 15 January 1915.

In March 1915 some of the 1st/4th Hampshires were sent to Basra, including Second Lieutenant E. Burrell, brother of Godfrey Burrell. In May and June the climate, particularly the moist heat in what is now Iraq but was then called Mesopotamia, was making itself felt. Some 180 men of the Hampshires were in hospital with heatstroke, six men died and eighty-four were invalided back to India to recover.

Because the campaign in Mesopotamia was going well, 200 reinforcements arrived from the Territorial Battalions in India in September 1915 and another 237 men arrived in October. The 2nd/4th Hampshires were still in India and carried out frontier training until the spring of 1916 when seventeen officers and 700 men were sent to Palestine (now Israel) where they stayed for almost a year.

Meanwhile, the 1st/4th Battalion of the Hampshires were still engaged in Mesopotamia, and between December 1916 and January 1917 they were south of Kut.

—— A LETTER HOME … WHICH WAS NEVER DELIVERED ——

Pte A. Worthington, 1987 H Company, 1st/4th Hants Regt, Indian Expeditionary Force, c/o Presidency Postmaster, Bombay, India, March 16 [19]15

My darling Mother,

Just a line hoping you are all well. I am except my face that's troubling me again; it's not very bad. I'm writing this on the boat on the way to the Persian Gulf. By what I hear we shall be fighting in a few days as we arrive on the 17th. Give my love to Alice & Annie and all at home. I do hope to see you all again someday. This is not a bad ship and the food not at all bad. We left India on Saturday, 13th March. I hope Mel [?] is better. We have all got a new rifle and bayonet each, so dear Mother the 4th Hants will do a bit of damage if we get near those Turkish devils. I think there are a lot of regular soldiers up there as well.

Well dear Mother & Dad, don't worry about me if you don't get a letter, goodness knows when I shall be able to write again. We just missed the mail when we left Pindi, so I can't say when I shall get your letter, but do write to me often wouldn't you. I expect we shall get the letters some when, now goodbye and god bless you.

Your ever-loving son, Alf

PS Dear Mother I have had to make a paper out […] to say who is my next of kin. You see Dad is, but that won't make anything different to you dear, because dear if anything do happen to me they will let Dad know. But Mother the money and all that's at home belonging to me, is yours if anything do happen. But there, you & Dad can settle that alright.

God Bless you all.

Your loving son, Alf X X X X X

The Hampshires were struck by sickness and reduced to some 150 of all ranks before they were involved in an attack on Turkish trenches south of Nasiriya in Mesopotamia on 24 July 1915. Nine officers and men were killed, including Alfred Worthington, and thirty-seven were wounded. However, the operation was considered a success as the Turkish positions were overcome, 1,000 prisoners were taken, 2,000 Turks were wounded and fifteen guns were captured. Nasiriya was occupied without further fighting and Major Burrell won the Military Cross for his role during this fierce encounter.

ALTON TROOPS LEAVING

Farewell to the Seaforth Highlanders and Black Watch.

Today (Saturday) the 7th Battalion Seaforth Highlanders and the 8th Battalion Black Watch are due to leave Alton for Bordon Camp. The regiments have been billeted in the town since 16 January and during that time the relationship between all ranks and the people of Alton has been of the most friendly character possible. Nothing could have exceeded that what has existed – the men have been well behaved in every way and they have gone out of their way in many instances to show their appreciation of any little kindness that may have been shown to them. They have fully appreciated all that has been done for them in the many reading and writing rooms and recreation halls in the town, and it is with a sincere feeling of regret that the town parts with them.

The men are going to Bordon to fire a musketry course prior to leaving for the front. We are sure that the townspeople wish them the best of luck in all the struggles on the continent that may be before them. They have been a blessing for the town in many ways and they will be greatly missed. As far as is known at present no regiments are coming to take their place.

HH&AG, 20 March 1915

In the event, the troops left on Sunday, 21 March 1915 and, whilst there do not seem to have been any more long-term deployments of troops to the area, odd detachments passed through and made occasional overnight stays.

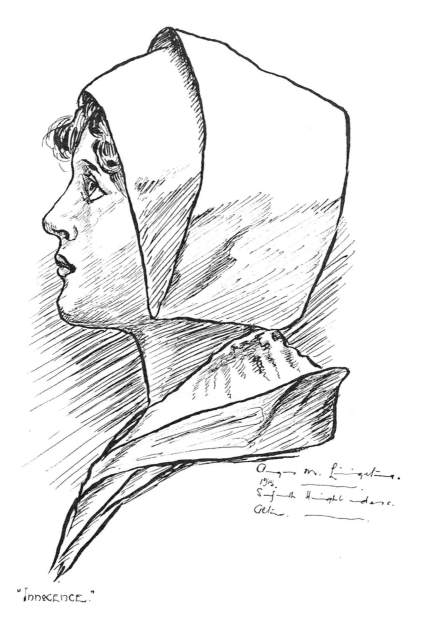

23. 'Innocence' – a pen and ink sketch of a young woman, drawn in the autograph book of a local lad early in 1915 by Angus Livingstone, Seaforth Highlanders.

————— BILLETS FOR THE TROOPS —————

Those responsible for the Alton Church of England School were not so pleased by the continued presence of the troops in the town and, at a meeting on 2 February 1915, they considered what could be done for the children whilst the schools were occupied by the army.

They agreed to write to the chairman of Hampshire County Council and the chairman of the Education Committee, pointing out that 'for the past 9 weeks or more the Alton Church of England and Council Schools had been occupied by the Military for the purposes of billeting troops and that it was impossible to carry on the education of the children'. They 'urged them that every possible step be taken in event of fresh troops being billeted in the town to save at least one of the larger schools from being used so that the Education of the children may be resumed'.

A meeting on 6 April 1915 reported that:

Since the Schools had been vacated by the Seaforth Highlanders the rooms had been fumigated and most of the walls washed down with disinfectant, but scrubbing the floors had not been carried out as other troops were being billeted there for the night. Arrangements had originally been made to reopen on 6 April, but this had not been possible, so they would now open on Monday, 12 April 1915.

————— LAST WORDS —————

In August 2013, wills made by servicemen from England and Wales who died in the Great War were released into the public domain on a Government Probate Service website. There appear to be some thirty or so examples from Alton men who died in the Great War.

The wills were the property of the War Office. They were often made the night before an attack and were written on a pre-printed page torn from their pay book. Most are as brief as the example below:

In the event of my death I give the whole of my property and effects to my wife Mrs F. Page, No. 4 Spitalfields, Alton, Hants, England 31/5/17

Most are accompanied by an official War Office form, which states that:

The enclosed document dated [*date added*] and signed [*name added*] appears to have been written by the person named in the margin [*of the form*] while he was 'in actual military service' within the meaning of the Wills Act, 1837, and has been recognised by the War Department as constituting a valid will.

Nationally, some 5 per cent of these are accompanied by final farewells to mothers, wives and sweethearts but these were never forwarded. Two undated Alton examples are:

7803 Pte H. White, A Company, 1st Hants Regt, Hyderabad Barracks, Colchester, Essex

Dear Jenny,

Just a few lines to you hoping you are quite well as it leaves me alright. There are 6 Divisions to go off to Belgium – we are waiting to go any moment – we are in the 4th Division out of the 6 Divisions under Lord Kitchener.

I suppose you have read who is in command of the British troops. We have been to Dover around the coast one day and a night and are just come back to base and we could hear the guns of the ships ponging away, especially the mines which the Germans had laid. The German fleet are pretty near done for & the reason we are not gone to Belgium yet is that the ships are busy [dredging] for mines so that we can get across the Channel, it means a clear sweep out for the Germans. The Belgians are waiting for the British troops to come to help them. We have here about 20 rounds.

Well Jenny, I will have to close, hoping to see you all again. I have left everything to you, my quarters money to come; you will get that if I don't get back. I must close, give my love to all.

Leonard

The 1st Hampshires, a Regular Army unit, arrived in Le Harve on 22 August 1914. They travelled by train to the front line near La Cateau and assisted in the retreat of the BEF from Mons. They then helped defend the line south of Ypres over the autumn and winter of 1914–15 and the regimental history mentions the high standard of trench cleanliness, comfort and defensibility of their zone – the Hampshires providing a model of what trenches could be like. However, trench foot, rheumatism, bronchitis and frostbite all posed a problem and, early in 1915, an officer and eleven men were killed in action. On 22 January 1915, Private White died in Etreat, a small seaside town, 25km north of Le Harve, where a hospital had been established in December 1914.

On 29 March 1915, the 2nd Hampshires sailed from Avonmouth for Gallipoli, via Egypt. Harry Pink wrote a quick letter home:

Pte H. Pink, 2nd Hampshire Regt, 83 Brigade, 29 Division, c/o GPO London

I am very sorry to tell you that we are moving shortly on active service so I wish you all good [luck], I hope you will be all right. It's with a good [heart] for I don't want you to worry over me and I made my will to you in case I never return back to England but I hope you will let me have a letter some time or another to let me know that you are all in good health and also let [Nell] know that I am out doing my duty. I am sorry that I can't write to her as I do not have her address. Dear Mother, I heard from Arthur and he tells me that they are on a move and I do hope that he will not have to come to the Front for I think it will be too hard for you if you lose us all for I don't expect ever I shall come back to see you any more after I get out there.

I think I have said all for this time so I am wishing you all goodbye.

From your ever loving son Harry x x x x x x
Please give my love to Florrie

On 25 April 1915, SS *River Clyde* (with Harry on board) landed on V Beach at Cape Helles and endured the worst of all the landings on that day. Harry Pink was wounded and evacuated from the area but died in hospital in Egypt on 20 May 1915.

Three months later, his brother Arthur was killed in the same campaign, whilst a third brother, Edward, was killed on the Somme the following year.

―――――― HAVE WE FORGOTTEN THE 4TH HANTS? ――――――

For several weeks now most of the letters from our Territorials in India are loud in their complaints that Alton has forgotten the men who have gone forth to do their duty on the Indian frontier. Have we forgotten the 4th Hants?

The feeling, no doubt, is a natural one for men, many of whom have left home for the first time. But the accusation that in entertaining the regiments which have been billeted in the town we have forgotten our own men, is hardly a fair one. India is a long way off. A letter often takes about six weeks to reach the hill stations at which the men are quartered, and it must feel a bit lonesome to get news of our doings which must be six weeks old before they are received. Then there is also the difficulty of knowing in which way it can be best shown that we have still our own men in our thoughts.

There is no use in sending comforts to men who are beginning to feel the heat of an eastern sun, and tobacco and cigarettes are, we believe, cheaper in India than they are at home. The fact is, even if we wish to send something we don't know what to send. Were the 4th Hants in France we are sure that the complaint we had forgotten them would never have been raised.

We have not forgotten them. We honour them for the work they are doing, and we will show it when we get a chance.

HH&AG, 3 April 1915

SS *FALABA*

SS *Falaba* sailed with 151 passengers and ninety-five crew from Liverpool bound for Sierra Leone on 27 March 1915. The following day, some 36 miles south-west by west of the Smalls Lighthouse off St David's Head in Wales, she sighted a submarine flying the White Ensign. However, as the submarine approached, it exchanged its flag for the German naval ensign.

The captain of the *Falaba* attempted to outrun the U-boat at 15 knots, but with a top speed on the surface of over 16 knots, *U-28* was slightly faster. The ship stopped and started lowering boats in anticipation of an attack. Only five boats had been prepared when *U-28* fired a torpedo from only 150yds, striking the *Falaba* amidships. Merely ten minutes later she had sunk and 104 of those on board died as a result. Amongst these was Sydney Monger from Alton, who was employed by Southern Nigerian Government Telegraphs. The SS *Falaba* has the dubious distinction of being the first unarmed passenger liner to be sunk during the Great War.

As submarines of the time had limited space for torpedoes, it was the practice for U-boats to surface and sink 'easy targets' with gunfire. The Royal Navy countered this by arming harmless-looking decoy ships, known as Q-ships, and using hidden guns to engage U-boats on the surface. On 22 March 1916, HMS *Farnborough* (Q-5) sank *U-68* in this way and used depth charges for the first time to ensure the destruction of the enemy submarine. Her commander, Gordon Campbell, was awarded the Victoria Cross. Following a similar action when he was commanding HMS *Dunraven* – which was sunk by *UC-71* on 8 August 1917 – two crewmembers were awarded VCs. Following his death in 1953, Vice Admiral Gordon Campbell VC DSO was buried in All Saints' churchyard in nearby Crondall.

CAPTAIN LANCELOT URQUHART UNWIN

Captain Lancelot Urquhart Unwin was born in China in 1883. He was the second son of Francis S. Unwin, the Commissioner of Customs in Shanghai; the grandson of Major-General Charles Herbert Unwin of the Indian Army; and a direct descendant of Mary Unwin, friend of the poet William Cowper.

Captain Unwin was educated at Berkhamstead in Montreux, Switzerland, and at the Royal Military College, Sandhurst, from which he was gazetted to the Hampshire Regiment in April 1903. He served with the Aden Hinterland Expedition of 1903–04, after which he was invalided with malarial fever. In December 1905 he became lieutenant, he was assistant adjutant of his battalion in 1907–08, captain in August 1911 and qualified as a Chinese interpreter in 1913.

Captain Unwin joined the BEF in September 1914 but was invalided home the following month after being wounded. He rejoined his battalion in December 1914 and served at the front until his death in the Second Battle of Ypres, on 27 April 1915. Captain Unwin was mentioned in Sir John French's despatch of 31 May 1915, for 'gallant and distinguished service in the field'. He was a relative of Miss Unwin of Westbank, Alton.

GALLIPOLI

Between 25 April 1915 and 9 January 1916, the British and French attempted to capture Constantinople (now Istanbul) from the Turkish Army. The operation would have secured a necessary sea route to Russia but it ended in failure with heavy casualties on both sides. The Australian and New Zealand Army Corps (ANZAC) took part in this campaign and it was their first major part in the war, often considered to mark the birth of national consciousness in both Commonwealth countries. Anzac Day (25 April) is still commemorated in memory of military casualties and veterans in these two countries.

PRIVATE L. CHESTERFIELD DROWNED

We have to record with great regret the first casualty among the H Company, 1st /4th Hants who are doing duty in the Persian Gulf. News was received on Thursday morning that Private Leonard Chesterfield, the youngest son of Mr T. Chesterfield of Alton, had been drowned while bathing.

The only consolation [to his family] is that he died while in the duty of his country, like thousands more of the pick of English manhood. Pte Chesterfield joined shortly after the outbreak of war. He was at the time serving his apprenticeship as a dentist in Winchester, and went to India with three of his brothers. He was a young man of considerable promise, and was well known and very popular in the town. For some years he was a prominent member of the Excelsior Football Club and was a keen athlete. He was 21 years of age.

HH&AG, 15 May 1915

FREDERICK GEORGE SUMNER

Alton Airman Killed – Promising Career Cut Short.

Baptised at All Saint's Church on 23 December 1888, Frederick George Sumner was the son of Henry (a gardener) and Annie of Ackender Terrace, Alton. He was killed in a flying accident on the East coast on Sunday, 14 May 1915.

The deceased showed a strong mechanical bent at an early age and when 15 was apprenticed to the engineering profession at the Alton paper mills, where he remained for 6 years. After gaining further experience in motor engineering with well-known firms, he became Inspector at the Royal Aircraft Factory, Farnborough. He was transferred to the Aeronautical Inspection Department following its formation at Farnborough by the War Office.

Showing ability and zeal, he was promoted to Chief Examiner and for some time had been based in Norfolk* in charge of the testing and inspection of machines, including the one in which he met his death. He was not piloting the machine which apparently hit a tree and crashed throwing him clear of the wreckage, but sustaining a fractured skull.

The funeral took place at All Saints' Church where the deceased had been a member of the choir from boyhood. There was a numerous attendance and a large number of wreaths, including floral tributes from various branches of the Royal Flying Corps.

HH&AG, 21 May 1915

MORE TROOPS IN TOWN

Alton was the scene, on Thursday and Friday evenings, of another of the stirring sights of wartime, when troops were again billeted in the town. On Thursday the RFA [Royal Field Artillery] attached to the 25th Division, stopped in the town and were billeted in private houses. They were on the march from Winchester to Fleet. The Infantry followed yesterday (Friday). It was quite like old times to see the streets filled with khaki. The weather was gloriously fine and the men looked fit and well after their hard winter's training.

The work of the Police in finding billets for so many men was hampered in many instances by people placing quite unnecessary obstacles in the way and refusing on the slightest pretext to take a soldier. We cannot understand the attitude of residents. They must be devoid of any spark of patriotism of national feeling. These men are defenders of the country and but for their self-sacrifice

---

* Probably in Norwich where Boulton & Paul began to construct aircraft under contract in 1915.

24. The Rolfe family created a composite photograph of their serving relatives. Percy (second
from the left) died in Gallipoli in 1915.

we should probably be in the same position as Belgium by now. Surely there are
few people who would not put themselves out a little to do the honour to men
who are giving up so much for the sake of their country. The Police, we are glad
to say, took a firm stand in the matter and issued a notice under the *Emergency
Billeting Act* saying that any persons who neglected or refused to take soldiers
after sufficient notice was given would on summary caution be liable to a fine
of not less than £2.

HH&AG, 29 May 1915

Interestingly, the logbook for the National School (now St Lawrence Primary
School) noted that, in the week ending 28 May 1915: 'Many girls have absented
themselves this week to help their mothers who have had soldiers billeted in
their houses.'

———— ALTON AND THE MAKING OF WAR MUNITIONS ————

After details of the foundries had been sent, Mr Geo. M. Booth wrote that
Alton and the work suggested were not suited for the making of munitions
of war. In a second letter it was pointed out that the Paper Mill was available
and might be of use in some direction but the Council was advised to apply
to some of the contractors of other materials if they wanted the mill utilised.
The Council agreed not to proceed further in the matter.

HH&AG, 29 May 1915

THE DARDANELLES LANDING

Pte Percy Rolfe, of the RMLI [Royal Marines Light Infantry], one of the five sons of Mr T. Rolfe, of Victoria Road, Alton, who was wounded at the Dardanelles and is at present recovering in Deaconess Hospital in Alexandria, writes a graphic and thrilling account of his experiences to Mr A. W. Caesar, the Headmaster of the Alton Council School, of which he is an old boy. It will be remembered that Pte Rolfe gave a very interesting account of his experiences in the defence of Antwerp after his return from that expedition. He writes:

'At present I am out of action, but hope soon to be on my feet again, but not like so many of my comrades, burning to be back in the fray, but when I go my heart and spirits will be as stout and as bold as any of them. As far as the Censor will permit me, I will give you an account of our fight with the Turks, and in doing so, let me say that I am not dreaming in a coat of shining armour. We want our friends to know what things are like out here, so that they may bear the burden as bravely as possible, for I know that there are a good many of the men from Alton and district out here who will never return.

We landed on a beautiful Wednesday evening [28 April 1915], just as the sun was setting over the large hill to our front. We were taken from our transport by torpedo-boat destroyers, and having been taken as near land as was safe for these craft, we were transferred to smaller pulling boats known as cutters, and holding anything from 15 to 40 men. We then pulled in shore and beached the boats, and quickly formed up in order. The Australians, who had landed the previous Sunday under the protection of the battleships, had got a foothold (at a cost), so making our landing easier, and we lost no one in landing. Owing to the opposition the Colonial troops met with, it was necessary for them to chase the Turks up the hill with the bayonet, and they were rather mixed up afterwards. We were ordered to relieve them to give them a rest and chance to reorganise.

We were provided with a guide, and were warned that German officers were sending in all kinds of false messages to the troops, for example, "No one is to fire until further orders. Stop firing on the right (or left). Don't fire, we are your supports" and all sorts of tricks. But we were up to them and when they tried that they would get double or more than they otherwise would. By daylight we had relieved the troops, and they were sent down the hill for a rest. The Turks seemed to know who we were and tried several tricks. They dressed in Colonial troops' uniforms and tried to break through our line, delivering an attack about noon, which failed. Then for two hours they shelled us heavily with but little effect, and then a great shell from one of the battleships seemed to take the go out of their gunners for a while, causing them to shift their batteries. As the night came on they tried another attack, but were received as before. The losses were heavy on both occasions, although until now ours had been light. They worried us all night, and at dawn shelled us heavily again, causing damage in our lines; the extent of the damage I must not disclose, but as they numbered about nine to our one they were thinned out more than we were.

Of course, you must expect to hear of barbarous fighting here, as they are being driven on by German officers, and you know from accounts of the fighting on the other fronts what heathen methods they are adopting. As our men are being taken down the ravine by the stretcher-bearers, who are in no way armed, they were shot at by snipers, who found their mark more often than they missed it. The field dressing stations were continually shelled, so heavily at times that the badly wounded could not be got down to the beach prior to being sent on board hospital ships.

A sniper had a shot at me one morning, but missed me by inches. I was trying to boil a can of water on a fireplace made of a few large stones, and one particular one the size of a saucer was struck and split clean in half. After that I chose another position for my fireplace very quickly! I was angry as I had just got a nice fire going. Anyway the Turk objected, and as he was not a man to argue fair and expose himself to me, I obliged him by moving.

Rifle fire and shelling all the day up to 5 p.m. was the day's programme, and then the Turks tried another attack. This time we expected them to finish off with a mad charge, but they finished very weakly and again fell back with less than they started with. One thing I have noticed about them is that they seem to dispose of their dead very quickly under cover of darkness.

The night passed quietly. I was present at the burial of one of my comrades. The service was conducted amid the noise of the guns and rifle fire, the scene lit up by a beautiful moon. It was a most impressive sight.

The next day (Saturday) the enemy were directly dropping shells into the trenches on our right for at least an hour; then they ceased. We knew then that their infantry were going to deliver an attack. Reinforcements were asked for as the Turks were attacking in great numbers, and as fast as they fell they were replaced. On they came, the thin line holding them in hand. 'Ten rounds rapid, fix bayonets, and standby' came the order from our Colonel, and 'Open out like a fan when you get out of the trench'. But whether the enemy saw the white flashing steel or what they knew, anyway they turned and ran, and things eased down a bit. We had been on the go from Wednesday, and it was Sunday before we got down the hill for a rest. Sleep being impossible you can guess we were about tired. All uphill work and having to make a footing complete in an enemy's country was none too easy. The great drawback is lack of water, which could not be obtained on land. Ours was sent from the ships, and we had to husband it and use it very sparingly. During the day the heat was intense, but the nights were very cold indeed. Our men were as bright and cheerful as if they were on their way home for a week. They made new dugouts and eased their boots; washing was out of the question. Having made a temporary home, they rested for the afternoon, and towards evening a sniper was seen having a few pot shots. He was stalking behind some bushes about 1,500 yards away [1,385m] on the side of a hill opposite. A party set out to chase him, but he did not wait for them; he moved very sharply indeed.

As dark came on we tucked in our rabbit holes for the night as we thought, but it was about 11.30 p.m. we were called out quietly, and being already equipped, fell in and marched off without a word. We guessed we were in for a night picnic. After marching up a most steep pass, very narrow and thick with mud and dead cattle, we arrived at the bluff of a hill. The maxim [machine gun] and rifle fire was terrible, and it was so difficult to get the wounded down, as the way was so narrow. Men were falling all about us. My rifle was shattered above the lower band and the wood cover stripped off. Our brave Colonel could only see one course, as the maxim fire was doing fearful destruction, and standing half way up the hill he shouted, 'Fix bayonets!' This being done, we cheered for the cause and on we rushed to shift the maxim or die. I shall never forget it to my dying day. I cannot think how a man like our Colonel could live in such a hell. I next felt a thud in my left thigh and I knew as I fell that I was 'out', and was losing blood rapidly. I remember very little as I only seemed to see troops pouring forward and a long line of glittering steel. I was taken down to the first field dressing station, and after a while was sent on to the Base Hospital, from where I was shifted on board the hospital ship. The same evening I was told the position was in

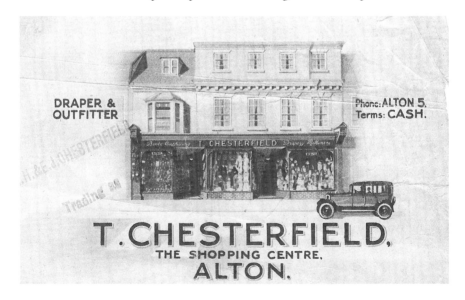

25. Billhead from T. Chesterfield's shop in the High Street. Two of his sons, died in the Great War.

English hands. I was awfully tired and slept soundly through the night, although shells frequently dropped near the ship, which bore Red Cross lamps on her side. She shifted several times out of range. Of course, I could expect no other than to hear that the Colonel had been killed, but to my intense delight I learned that he was only wounded and on board the hospital ship, and after a few hours we were talking to one another, master and servant wondering how the other had been spared. I was sent to Alexandria, and am now in a beautiful hospital built by the Germans and bagged by the British Government.'

HH&AG, 12 June 1915

Private Rolfe seems to have recovered and returned to Gallipoli where he died on 13 July 1915 during the action of Achi Baba Nullah. Percy Rolfe is commemorated on the Helles Memorial, which serves the dual function of a Commonwealth battle memorial for the whole Gallipoli campaign and a place of commemoration for many of those Commonwealth servicemen who died there and have no known grave.

ALTON SEES MORE OF THE ARMY

Alton saw something of the Army again on Thursday – in fact there were more soldiers about in the evening than have ever been seen in Alton on one night since the war started. A whole division was bivouacked in the district around

26. The Union Jack Club, a recreational facility for off-duty soldiers, is thought to have been located in Normandy Street, Alton, during the Great War.

Alton from Chawton to Holybourne Downs. They reached the town from Basingstoke soon after 10 in the morning, and thousands poured through, dusty, bronzed, but radiantly happy Irishmen. Many of the regiments had bands playing, and the boys could whistle! In the evening it would have been possible almost to have walked on their heads along the high Street. They formed part of an Irish Division [between 10,000 and 15,000 men] to which one of the Hampshire battalions is attached, and Alton has never seen a finer body of troops.

HH&AG, 19 June 1915

MOBILISING THOSE LESS ABLE

The Rt Hon. D. Lloyd George, Minister of Munitions, has sent the following message to the lads undergoing training at the Lord Mayor Treloar Cripples' College, Alton who are at present engaged on a War Office contract for soldiers' greatcoat straps.

It has given me much pleasure to hear that the boys of the Treloar Cripples' Hospital and College are anxious to help their country in every way possible, and as Minister of Munitions I wish to express to them my personal appreciation of the zeal and enthusiasm with which they are carrying on the work which has been entrusted to them.

HH&AG, 26 June 1915

TOBACCO FUND FOR THE SEAFORTHS AND BLACK WATCH

The local fund for sending tobacco to the Seaforth Highlanders and Black Watch, who were billeted in the town, does not make much progress, due we believe to the fact that personal parcels are being sent out by friends of the soldiers. Mr Bernard Johnson is still keeping the list open. It is necessary to get £5 before a parcel will be sent direct, and we hope Alton people generally will not forget the men who were such great favourites when they were here. Mr A. Piper is also collecting, and a collecting card is also hung in the Constitutional Club.

HH&AG, 26 June 1915

THE DEVASTATION OF WAR

Lance Corporal Henry Faithfull of Holybourne, wrote in the early summer of 1915 from what appears to be the area around Ypres in Belgium:

An Explanation
and a Request

The smokes in this parcel have been subscribed for by supporters of the Sailors' and Soldiers' Tobacco Fund in all parts of the World, as a testimony of their kindly feelings towards the cause of the Allies.

They would naturally be glad to hear from you of the safe arrival of the parcel, and would treasure a memento in the shape of a few words from the men who are "making history."

So will you please be sure and return this postcard? It needs no stamp—just a few words from you on the back, and the Sailors' and Soldiers' Tobacco Fund will see that the donor (whose name is on the back) receives the postcard in due course.

Sailors' and Soldiers'
Tobacco Fund
Central House, Kingsway,
W.C.

165

POST CARD.

To F. HOWARD TYAS, Esq.
Managing Secretary,
Sailors' and Soldiers' Tobacco Fund,
Central House,
Kingsway,
London, W.C.,
England,

27. Soldiers' and Sailors' Tobacco Fund postcard.

I am in dugouts, not far from the firing line. I hope soon we shall go back for a rest. I am sitting just opposite the places I told you to read about. The Cathedral and churches are knocked about fearfully. There are houses close to our dugout here where we get our water. I went across last night to get some and had a look around. There's a grandfather clock standing in one room, still going, so I suppose someone still winds it up. There are a lot of religious things over houses and what we see a lot of out here is Christ on the Cross, in a little glass case. There are a lot of good things left about in the houses that are part knocked down. It does seem a shame. A fellow from another regiment shot a cow this morning and cut it up. You ought to have seen the fellows coming back with handfuls of it to cook. I didn't have any as I didn't fancy it. The sun is shining now on that Cathedral and shows it up more even though it is simply a mass of ruins. One place was burning over a week. There's a little village on the right of me as I sit here writing, only about 200 yards [185m] away. There's a church there all smashed to pieces, also the graveyard. Yet last night they were pitching shells into it, two or three at a time. Talk about noise! We had to get out of the way under cover.

We are now resting. Its ten o'clock and we have just come off parade. We had to parade at 9.30 for inspection of rifles, ammunition, respirators, boots cleaned and everyone shaved. Our platoon officer inspected us but this afternoon the General inspects us. It is a game getting ready for it, I can tell you. I went and bought four eggs for 7*d* [about 3p] yesterday and had them for tea – two for my mate and two for myself and they went down jolly good. After tea I watched a game of quoits; they were made out of horseshoes. A German aeroplane came over and our anti-aircraft guns fired at it but it got away. An aeroplane is one of the hardest things to hit.

We moved away at five o'clock this morning and we were on the march till a quarter to eight. It was hot too; my things were wet through with perspiration. We were up at half-past three, had some tea and a slice of bread and jam, got our place cleared up and ready to start at five. It seems very thundery here. We are close to the wood where we were before, in some short trenches meant for dugouts, I suppose. It's a rotten place this time. I don't know how long we are here for, but I shouldn't be surprised to be in the trenches tonight. We had some breakfast after we got here – they gave us some raw bacon and my mate went to the cooker and got it fried, so we had rashers for breakfast. We do live [well] out here, don't we? But I would like to get hold of a good square meal for a treat. If we do stay here tonight we shall have the sky for a roof. All right if it's fine, but not much if it rains. That's the best of being in the barn. I thought it was too good to last, but never mind, we have all got to make the best of it.

Sunday. Here I am in the trenches; another Sunday in them. We are now in some French trenches, some the Germans drove them out off by gas, and then the French took them again; so you can tell they are knocked about. We have plenty of work at night, filling sandbags to make them up. We usually start at ten o'clock. We 'stand to' at two o'clock in the morning for an hour. After that the rum ration is served out, and letters and parcels then. It is only about three tablespoonfuls of rum; of course I don't take any. There are lots of dead been buried close to here. I don't suppose they had time to bury them properly. It seems a shame, doesn't it? I have seen some mud in my time, but never anything like this. It was fine when we started Friday night for the trenches and it's kept fine since, which is a good job. We had to cross the canal and of course they were shelling it. The shells killed three and wounded one as they came across, not our regiment though. The bridge we came across is blown up now, I believe. All along the canal are lots of trees; dozens of them are knocked down and blown about. In peacetime it must be a lovely place; now there's nothing but desolation. Just the other side of the canal we got into a communications trench and well we know it too. We started by getting into water up to our ankles, and by the time it was finished, it was over my knees, so I don't know how the short fellows would fare. My word it was in a mess. I had my coat on so you can guess what that was like. Some of the fellows changed their socks when they got into the trench, but I didn't, and I'm glad I didn't, for I was sent down to headquarters with some men for some sandbags. HQ was nearly at the end of the communications trench. There wasn't so much water and mud there, but it was up to my knees. I did change my socks this morning as my feet hurt so; the mud had dried on so I couldn't get them off and had to cut them from my feet. The trench where we are is quite dry; in places it's rotten.

Where we are the Germans are 100 yards [92m] away, but in some places it's only 25 yards [23m]. It's been fairly quiet although they do a good deal of sniping. What they seem to use mostly are hand grenades and trench mortars – like a small gun in the trench. They don't make as much row as some of the shells, but they don't do so much damage, and another thing is you can see them coming and can dodge them. At night you can see a little light coming through the air and in the daytime the thing itself. We had two fellows killed and one wounded this morning by one of them. Another of our fellows had his hand shot right along his fingers and he will have to lose two or three of his fingers; a sniper did it. Our company officer got hit on the arm with a piece of one of those trench mortars. I shall be glad of the parcel, for we only got three loaves between eleven men this morning. But they gave us a piece of bacon, and I was surprised that it was a real good piece too.

Tuesday. I hear we are to be relieved tomorrow night, to go back a little way in dugouts. I would sooner stay here, for the dugouts are by the canal and they keep shelling it to destroy the bridges the Engineers have put up for the troops to cross. The Germans started to use a small searchlight last night. Of course both sides fire lights [flares] from pistols, but that's the first time I've seen them use a searchlight. They only had it on a few minutes as we all fired at it. They didn't show it afterwards; probably they thought an attack was coming off, or something.

My word, it is hot today. We can see that town I told you of in the distance. Tho' we are a different side of it to what we were last time. I can see the towers. Did I tell you the hops out here go up straight strings, not slanting ones as at home. Before we came into the trenches we were close to a British gun, a monster. Sometimes you see in the paper 'Nothing to report but artillery duels'. Yes, that's all right but it's the infantry who have to put up with that tho'.

HH&AG, 26 June 1915

LIEUTENANT EDWARD ARNOLD DYER

Lieutenant Edward Arnold Dyer, the son of Edward and Annie Laurie of Hastings, was born on 22 July 1873 at Alton, Hants. He was educated at Brighton College, became a solicitor and married Barbara, with whom he had two children: Arnold (1907) and Alexander (1911). He served in the Boer War and went to Canada, returning on the outbreak of war to be appointed second lieutenant of the

9th Kings Light Shropshire Infantry and was attached to the Border Regiment in Gallipoli. He was killed in action on 28 June 1915 and buried in Twelve Tree Copse Cemetery.

ANOTHER ALTON DEATH IN MESOPOTAMIA

We regret to record the death of another Alton lad with the H Co., 1/4 Hants. News was received in Alton this week of the death from enteric fever on the hospital ship *Madras* of Pte Harold J. Brown [should be Bown], of H Coy, 1/4 Hants. The deceased was the adopted son of Mr & Mrs Twitchin of Inglewood, Alton, and he was only 20 years of age. The full facts of his death are not known, but it is evident from the information received that he contracted enteric fever while on duty in Mesopotamia, and died on board the hospital ship to which he was removed. Only a day or two before the news of his death arrived, a letter was received from him in which he said he had been in hospital with a slight attack of fever, but was now well again. The news naturally came as a great shock, and will be received with regret in the town where he was well known. Deceased was a clerk in the Union of London and Smith's Bank. He was formerly at the Winchester branch for a short while and at the outbreak of war was at Alresford branch and he had done relief duty at Alton on several occasions.

HH&AG, 3 July 1915

LIEUTENANT COLONEL CECIL HOWARD PALMER

Lieutenant Colonel Palmer was born on 14 July 1873 at Eastbourne, Sussex. On 28 November 1903, he married Miss Hilda Beatrice Hall, the eldest daughter of Mr and Mrs Gerald Hall of Anstey Manor, Alton, in St Lawrence church, Alton. Flags were displayed at the church, in the public square and at several other points in the town, and the church bells (both in Alton parish church and East Worldham) rang several merry peals in honour of the event.

On 26 July 1915, Palmer – commander of the 9th Battalion Royal Warwickshire Regiment – was killed in action near Hill Q in Gallipoli. He had served in the Boer War as aide-de-camp to General Aldershot Infantry Brigade in 1901–02, as adjutant in the 1st Worcestershire Volunteer Battalion in 1906–09, and he had also been a Hampshire County cricketer. His name appears on the Worcester Guildhall, Worcester St Peter's church and East Worldham church memorials.

HMS *LYNX*

HMS *Lynx*, a destroyer, entered service in 1913. She was serving with the 4th Destroyer Flotilla of the Grand Fleet based at Scapa Flow in Orkney and was lost after hitting a mine in the Moray Firth on 9 August 1915. From a crew of ninety-six, only twenty-six survived. Stoker First Class Thomas Pacey from Alton was among the casualties.

LOSS OF HMT *ROYAL EDWARD*

On 28 July 1915, HMT *Royal Edward* left for Gallipoli with 1,367 officers and men. After stopping at Alexandria in Egypt, she left for the island of Lemnos on 12 August. The following morning, however, the German submarine *UB-14* spotted her and sank the ship with a torpedo fired from about a mile away.

British hospital ship *Soudan* was in the vicinity and picked up the *Royal Edward*'s SOS. Some 440 men were rescued by the *Soudan*, and a further 221 were taken aboard two French destroyers and some trawlers, but between 132 and 935 men are reported to have died in the incident. On 5 September 1915, a newspaper report gave the number as 752, including 111 men of the 2nd Hampshire Regiment; Lance-Corporal William Hurlock of Alton amongst them.

28. Thomas Pacey was killed when HMS *Lynx* struck a mine and sank in the Moray Firth on 9 August 1915.

HMS *ATTENTIVE*

HMS *Attentive*, an Adventure class scout cruiser, formed part of the 6th Destroyer Flotilla patrolling around Dover. On 7 September 1915, *Attentive* was bombed by a German Albatross aircraft at Ostend. Two crewmembers were killed and seven were wounded. One of the wounded was Private Percy Giles, Royal Marine Light Infantry, of Alton who died six days later.

LIFE IN SHRAPNEL GULLY

Pte A.G. Arnold, 10th Hants, was a well-known Altonian and a member of the Church Lads' Brigade and the Alton Military Band. He wrote a letter home from the convalescent camp in Malta, where he was recovering from wounds that he received at the Dardanelles:

> I am just writing a few lines to let you know that I am still alive and kicking. I expect you have heard all about the Turks catching me bending on 9 August. I got hit on the right buttock and the left shoulder, but I am pleased to say that I am beginning to feel tip-top again. We landed at Anzac on 3 August and had a night or two in Shrapnel Gully. They call it by that name because the Turks plough the place with their Jack Johnsons* and then sow it with shrapnel. Well, we soon got orders to pack traps and be off after the Turks. We found ourselves out on the left by the Salt Lake, and then had to do the Turkey trot towards that little hill, 971. It was on the top of that that your humble got his dose. By the way the shot and shell was flying about you would not have thought a fly could have lived in it. Any man who got away with it was lucky, but God only knows what the Turks must have suffered. I have had a good time in hospital, and I can speak well of the doctors and staff. Everyone is so good and kind to you.
>
> Kindly remember me to all old pals.
>
> *HH&AG*, 16 October 1915

---

* The heavy, black German 15cm artillery shell was nicknamed 'Jack Johnson' after the Afro-American heavyweight boxing champion, Jack Johnson, on account of its power and the large amount of dark smoke given off by these big shell explosions.

—————————— A DESCRIPTION OF THE TRENCHES ——————————

Lieutenant Bernard Walter Bentinck of the 13th Battalion, Rifle Brigade in France, sent a number of letters home to his mother at Alton House in Alton:

I have no conception of the scale on which it has all been done, and this is, of course, only a small fraction of the line. One enters the trenches a long way behind the firing line, quite three quarters of a mile [*c.* 1,200m], I should think. They are about 6ft [1.8m] deep everywhere and just wide enough to allow two men to pass each other, and with the parapets on each side of sandbags and earth they are about 8ft [2.4m] deep from the bottom to the top of the parapet. There is a wooden seat about 2ft [60cm] or more off the ground, on which the men stand to shoot. All the sides are held up (it is nearly all clay) by fine meshed wire netting and other such things, with large pits for carrying off surface water every twenty yards [19m] or so. The men sleep in dugout holes cut in the walls of the trenches so that they lie straight out three or four together, and they cook all their own food on tiny fires of wood and coke in little niches along the sides, and I saw a lot of men whose steaks and potatoes smelt very appetising. I must have walked through miles of trenches yesterday, nearly all with floor boarding, like one has in the scullery for the maids to stand on; so except in unusually low places one need never get wet, but I expect it was very different a year ago. The dugouts where the officers live are in some cases very snugly furnished with stuff out of the houses, several of which stand as skeletons inside our lines, and are floored with coloured tiles in some cases. Every regiment makes it a point of honour to leave the trenches and dugouts as clean as they possibly can, and they can get quite fond of their special abodes. My companion and I sleep in a new one, just like a cabin with a bunk on each side and a passage down the middle. I could stand upright inside it, and the bed mattress of wire netting was quite comfortable.

HH&AG, 4 September 1915

My dugout has a roof of thick logs, about as thick as a man's leg, laid cross-ways, with earth and wire netting between, about 3ft [1m] altogether. Absolute protection from anything. The trenches are about 8ft [2.4m] deep where our private trench joins on to them, so one is absolutely safe while passing from trenches to dugout, and we are most comfortable inside. The walls are covered with straw laid on, then wired against the sides, and the beds are stakes driven into the ground, tops about 2ft [60cm] off the ground, joined by wood at the sides and ends with wirer netting stretched in between – a primitive but thoroughly comfortable wire mattress. The stove we have in one corner burns exceedingly well. It is about 18 inches [45cm] high and the chimney goes out through the roof.

Being in charge of the signallers, I am generally up around 4 a.m., and around the trenches to ask if anything of interest has taken place during the night, such as snipers observed, digging parties heard and so on. I get on to HQ about 5.45 and make out my report, which goes to the General by bicycle orderly, so that he gets it by 6.30 a.m. Then I get a wash and shave at the dressing station about 50 yards [45m] off and come back to HQ for breakfast at 7.30 a.m. After breakfast I have to check all the telephone stations are OK and in touch with one another, see the interpreter, who orders food etc. from the nearest town, and with one thing and another it is 12 before I am free. I walk at 1 p.m. to my dugout and we have lunch there, and I walk back to HQ, making a tour en route of all my signalling stations. All the letters for censoring come in during the day from 5 to 7 p.m. I am busy stamping them, and censoring those of my own men, and any others which I notice have not been properly dealt with. I generally walk up to my dugout before dinner to avoid the walk in the dark, and we have a most attractive supper there, and I turn in about 9. We are having real September weather, and quite beautiful it is – still and sunny days with a cloudless blue sky, and it is wonderful how in the middle of the day, say between 1 and 1.30, there is absolute silence along the line, not a shot being fired anywhere. One can hardly imagine that it is wartime and that one is in the heart of it. The birds are singing gaily outside my windows as I am writing this.

HH&AG, 18 September 1915

Born on 16 July 1877, Bernard Walter Bentinck was the son of Baron Walter Theodore Edward Bentinck and Henrietta Jane Christina Hinton. He graduated from and was admitted to Middle Temple, and was entitled to practice as a barrister. He gained the rank of captain, survived the war and died on 27 June 1931, aged 53.

– LIEUTENANT GILBERT EDWARD BURNEY – 'A FINE DEATH' –

Lieutenant Burney was born in Chester on 8 July 1891, the second son of Brigadier General H.H. Burney of Langham Lodge [now known as Barton End], Alton, CB, late Gordon Highlanders and his wife Diana Gertrude. He was educated at Clayesmore and Shrewsbury; went to Ceylon in 1912 and settled there as a Tea Planter but returned to England on the outbreak of war, obtained a Second Lieutenancy in the Gordon Highlanders on 17 October 1914 and was promoted Lieutenant on 26 March 1915. Appointed ADC to Major-General Landon CB, commanding the 9th Scottish Division. Went to France in May and took part in the Battle of Loos in September 1915 and died whilst serving in the 8th (Service) Battalion, the Gordon Highlanders, probably at Chocques on

27 September from wounds received in action near the Hohenzollern Redoubt the same day. He was unmarried.

His General wrote: 'I want you to know how splendid he was, and how much I am convinced his gallant and fearless example helped'; an Officer on the HQ Staff was quoted, 'He was, indeed, a most gallant lad, and keen to be up and doing, or in the trenches. It was a fine death; you may be well proud of him. I have written to … and asked him to do all he can to get his behaviour mentioned in *Despatches*. He deserved it thoroughly.'

An Officer in the 8th Gordon Highlanders also wrote, 'He was absolutely without fear. It is a fearful blow to all who knew him' and another, 'He was a lovable boy, and made friends everywhere, and he was also the most high-spirited I ever knew – a boy to be proud of.'

He was mentioned in Despatches by Field Marshal Sir John (now Lord) French [*London Gazette*, 1 January 1916] for conspicuous gallantry in the actions of 25-26-27 September [1915], and for gallantry and efficiency as Observation Officer when communications were cut several times.

Roll of Honour, p. 48

REMEMBERING THE SCOTS

Many Alton families who had Scottish soldiers billeted with them formed close attachments and, during the early part of the war, the *HH&AG* carried notes relating to their progress following the receipt of letters. Often the news was the death of an individual – 'Pte J.M. Smith, 7th Seaforth Highlanders, killed in action 16 August 1915, billeted at No. 8 Bow Street', published on 4 September 1915, and 'Corpl James McLean, 12th Royal Scots, killed in action 2 August 1915, formerly billeted at No. 90 High Street', published on 11 September 1915 – and at other times they were more general:

> The casualty lists which have been published during the last fortnight tell only too plainly how the gallant Scots who were billeted in Alton last winter have paid the price in the great advance. Many officers and men who spent several months in Alton lie now 'somewhere in France', their graves marked with a rough wooden cross. They died as heroes for their King and Country and Alton mourns their loss with pride.
>
> *HH&AG*, 23 October 1915

Pte J. Moore of the 8th Battalion Black Watch was billeted with Mr Hobbs of No. 1 Church Street, Alton. The 17-year-old sent what was described by the editor as a 'thrilling account' of his experiences in France:

I was in the big advance on 25–27 September and it was hot while it lasted. The night before my first bayonet charge everybody knew we were going over the parapet in the morning and we couldn't help thinking how we were going to fare, but everyone was cheery and didn't seem to be troubled about what the next day would bring. We got the order to 'stand to' at 5.15 a.m. and at 5.30 we got over. Our guide was a pithead nearly a mile away. Whether it had been left standing for that purpose I can't say, but between us and that pit was three lines of trenches and a redoubt that held many machine guns. We went through them like a football team of internationals playing a lot of schoolboys. Our officer was the first to fall before he got many yards over. As he fell he shouted for Sergeant Rogers, our platoon sergeant, and told him to take command and right well he did. He never troubled about himself, always shouting the direction to go next, every line of trenches we took. We went straight through until we came to a village with the Germans firing out of the houses up to the last minute and then they came out with their hands up. They went down on their knees in front of us shouting for mercy and turning out their pockets. Nearly every one of them was using those explosive bullets and I don't mind telling you it was their death warrant. We took a lot of prisoners and got another line of trenches through the village. There we had to stop as the Brigade on our left got held up amongst the barbed wire. We held on to what we had until we were relieved by fresh troops. We came right back to the trenches we started from. All next day the fighting was hot and on the Monday we had to go over to the help of those that relieved us. We were there until another Division came up. We came out of the trenches on the Tuesday morning and I can't tell you what we looked like. All our officers got either killed or wounded and I can't tell you how many men we lost. I am not telling you the sights I saw those days or how I felt, but the most of us never touched food from the Friday to the Tuesday. I came down from the trenches minus equipment, cap, waterproof sheet and [covered in] mud and water from head to foot. It was not the best of weather; it rained hard when we were in the last line of trenches and we were standing well over our knees in water. I was not sorry when we left, but we were on the march for another part of the line. So I am writing to you from the trenches again. Nearly all of my mates are killed or wounded and, as far as I believe, of the battalion that was billeted in Alton, very few are left of them.

HH&AG, 23 October 1915

Private Moore was killed on 29 April 1916.

Sergeant Charles Anderson of A Company, 8th Black Watch, had a whirlwind romance in Alton and, on 19 April 1915, he married Maud Collop, the daughter of the landlord of The Prince of Wales public house in Holybourne. Unfortunately, he died on 25 September 1915 during the Loos offensive:

29. Many of the Scottish soldiers who were billeted in Alton lost their lives in September 1915 around Loos in Northern France. The Loos Memorial is seen here in May 2013 and their names are amongst those remembered on 139 stone panels surrounding the cemetery.

I am very sorry to tell you that Sergt Anderson was reported wounded and missing after the heavy fighting near the Hohenzollern Redoubt on 25 September. I have delayed writing to you as I hoped to get news about him, but so far I have heard nothing. All his gun team were either killed or wounded, with the exception of one man; it has therefore been very difficult to get information; but when he was last seen he was alive, but rather badly wounded. Since then we have heard nothing. It would be wrong for me to encourage you to hope too much. I knew Sergt Anderson as a good soldier and a brave man, and he fought his gun well [*sic*]. I sympathise with you deeply in your loss.

Captain Duke, Gun Officer, 8th Black Watch

HH&AG, 23 October 1915

Sergeant Anderson's body was never recovered and he is remembered on the Loos Memorial, which forms the sides and back of Dud Corner Cemetery.

After the Great War, some Scottish soldiers with next of kin in Scotland had their names submitted by Alton families with whom they were associated, for inclusion on the plaque on the Alton War Memorial.

To date it has not been possible to determine the fate of Corporal Angus M. Livingstone of 7th Seaforth Highlanders who composed the Alton poem and drew the sketch of a young woman in the autograph book of an Alton youngster.

30. Handbill requesting donations for the troops at the front.

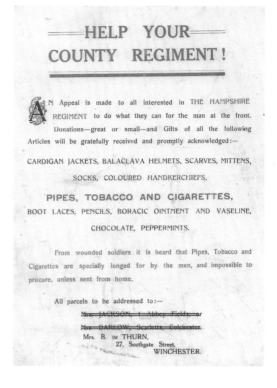

=== HELP YOUR ===
COUNTY REGIMENT !

AN Appeal is made to all interested in THE HAMPSHIRE
REGIMENT to do what they can for the man at the front.
Donations—great or small—and Gifts of all the following
Articles will be gratefully received and promptly acknowledged:—

CARDIGAN JACKETS, BALACLAVA HELMETS, SCARVES, MITTENS,
SOCKS, COLOURED HANDKERCHIEFS,

PIPES, TOBACCO AND CIGARETTES,
BOOT LACES, PENCILS, BORACIC OINTMENT AND VASELINE,
CHOCOLATE, PEPPERMINTS.

From wounded soldiers it is heard that Pipes, Tobacco and
Cigarettes are specially longed for by the men, and impossible to
procure, unless sent from home.

All parcels to be addressed to:—

~~Mrs. JACKSON, 1 Abbey Fields, or~~
~~Mrs. BARLOW, Scarletts, Colchester.~~
Mrs. B. im THURN,
27, Southgate Street,
WINCHESTER.

During his short stay in Alton in 1915, Corporal Robert McArthur of C Company, 7th Battalion Seaforth Highlanders seems to have got on well with one particular Altonian. In fact, when he was killed in Flanders on 1 October 1918, his next of kin included Jane McArthur of No. 46 Butts Road, Alton.

Another Scot, James Mackay, came back to Alton and married his sweetheart, Ellen Poore, at All Saints' church on 19 October 1918. Happily, he survived the end of the war.

—————— SERGEANT MAJOR JOHN FOSBURY ——————

Battery Sergeant Major John Fosbury was a regular soldier and his wife and four children lived at No. 7 Kingsland Road, Alton. His youngest daughter, Joan, was just 15 months old when her father died, on 5 November 1915.

She wrote in 2005, '… memories are so precious. My one big sorrow was never having a father and so many have suffered the same. What a brave mother we had.'

After her father was killed, the army offered her mother training as a midwife '… but it would have meant us children being cared for in army schools and she did not want to be parted from us. What hard decisions had to be made – we had a super mother and so many widows were left to make these decisions.'

31. Battery Sergeant Major Fosbury, a Regular Army soldier, in a relaxed mood, 1915.

32. Headstone of Battery Sergeant Major Fosbury in Philosophe British Cemetery, Pas de Calais, France, May 2013.

Joan was very proud of the fact that her father's battery included Bombardier Ernest George Horlock VC.

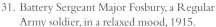

THE HORLOCKS

Ernest George Horlock was born at Beech Farm, Alton, although his family later moved to Langrish, then Littlehampton and his name is on the war memorial in both places. Ernest was so anxious to do his share of the fighting during the Battle of the Aisne on 15 September 1914, that he twice delayed obeying the doctor's orders when wounded. Officers subsequently learnt of his actions and he was taken to the doctor who made sure he was placed in hospital. Ernest was later promoted to sergeant and awarded the Victoria Cross for his devotion to duty. He was one of the few servicemen who actually received his award from the king himself.

Ernest remained with 113 Battery until February 1916 when he was promoted to battery sergeant major and posted elsewhere. He later served in Salonika and Egypt. Returning to Egypt after his marriage in Littlehampton in October 1917, the vessel

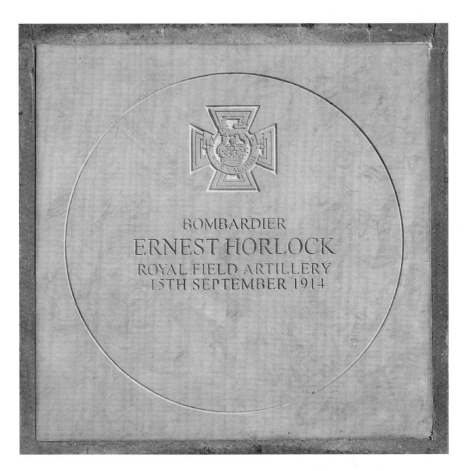

BOMBARDIER
ERNEST HORLOCK
ROYAL FIELD ARTILLERY
15TH SEPTEMBER 1914

33. Commemorative paving stones mark the 100th anniversary of the date that recipients of the Victoria Cross received their award. The paving stones appear all around the UK, in 454 communities. Bombardier Horlock's stone in Alton was the eighth to be unveiled.

he was on – HMT *Aragon* – was torpedoed on 30 December 1917 near Alexandria and sank. Although the destroyer HMS *Attack* rescued between 300–400 men, she was also hit by a torpedo and Horlock was one of 610 who were killed. His body was amongst those recovered and was buried in the British Military Cemetery at Hadra near Alexandria.

On 24 May 2001, a memorial was unveiled in St John's parish church, Langrish and, in Alton, he appears on a memorial stone behind the Cairn (pictured above).

His brother, John Harry Horlock (also born at Beech Farm, Alton), likewise served in the Great War. He was a private in the Dorset Regiment but died on 24 January 1916 during the Siege of Kut el Amara and was buried in Kut War Cemetery, Iraq. He is also listed on the Littlehampton War Memorial, although the Littlehampton town website indicates that they believed he was a resident of Alton.

GALLIPOLI DISASTER

In a laconic, single-sentence communiqué, the War Office in London this afternoon revealed that the ill-fated Gallipoli expedition had been abandoned after ten months of bad luck, muddle, indecisiveness and outstanding heroism by British, Australian and New Zealand troops.

The final act of evacuating some 90,000 men, with 4,500 animals, 1,700 vehicles and 200 guns, was carried out with great skill and ingenuity, under the very noses of powerful Turkish forces. Not a single life was lost. Some 30,000 beds had been prepared for the wounded in Mediterranean hospitals, but these were not needed.

The evacuation was carried out at night time. During the day, however, ships riding at anchor under Turkish observation could be seen disembarking troops and unloading guns and stores. The trick was that more men and materials were being evacuated during the night than had ostentatiously been brought ashore during the day.

In the last stages, at Anzac Bay, when it seemed the Turks could not fail to hear what was going on, a destroyer trained its searchlight on the enemy's trenches. While the Turks concentrated their fire on the destroyer, the troops were lifted off the beaches.

As the last men were leaving, having set thousands of booby traps, a huge landmine in no-man's-land was exploded. The Turks, thinking the Australians were attacking, began a furious barrage of fire that lasted forty minutes.

It was a better end than might have been expected to a sorry story that began when the Russians appealed to Britain and France for munitions. Ministers and military men in London agreed to let the Royal Navy try to get to Russia's Black Sea ports by forcing the passage of the Dardanelles; they also decided a back-up force of land troops would be needed.

Kitchener said he could not spare men from the Western Front. Three weeks later he changed his mind and said he could send a division to join Royal Marines and troops from Egypt.

But by the time the combined land and sea operation was mounted at the end of April, a full two months after the Navy first bombarded the Dardanelles forts, all advantage of surprise had been lost and the Turks had heavily reinforced their positions.

When Bulgaria* came into the war, a clear route was opened for Germany to keep Turkey supplied. Britain decided to pull out and use the men, as today's announcement says, in 'another sphere of operations'.

The Commons had been told that the casualties were 25,000 dead, 76,000 wounded, 13,000 missing and 96,000 sick admitted to hospital.

The Manchester Guardian, 20 December 1915

---

* Bulgaria entered the war on the enemy side on 15 October 1915.

Helles, at the south-western end of the Gallipoli peninsula, was retained for a period, but at the end of December it was decided to evacuate the garrison. Unlike the evacuation from Anzac Cove, Turkish forces were looking for signs of withdrawal and, having used the intervening time to bring up reinforcements and supplies, they mounted an attack on 7 January 1916 with infantry and artillery; the attack failed and heavy casualties were inflicted.

British troops laid mines with time fuses and that night, under the cover of a naval bombardment, they began to fall back 5 miles (8km) from their lines to the beaches, where makeshift piers were used to board boats. The early morning of 8 January 1916 saw the last British troops (numbering some 35,268) depart.

THE SINKING OF P&O LINER *PERSIA*

The P&O liner *Persia*, which left London on 13 December 1915 and Marseilles on 25 December bound for Bombay, was torpedoed by *U-38* off Crete at about 1.30 p.m. on 30 December. The vessel sank in five minutes. Only four boats got away and these were picked up by a steamer heading to Alexandria.

Among the passengers was Mr Arthur Russell Windham, son-in-law of Mr Gerald Hall of Anstey Manor, Alton. A civil engineer, he was on his way to take up a post with the Egyptian Government and perished with the ship. Mr Windham was in Alton shortly before he sailed and left a widow and two children, a boy and a girl, who lived in Rogate. This was the second bereavement Mr and Mrs Hall sustained within a few months, as another son-in-law, Lieutenant Colonel C.H. Palmer of the Worcester Regiment, was killed at Gallipoli in July 1915.

In breach of naval international law, the ship was not stopped and searched for contraband and neither were those on board put in a place of safety (for which lifeboats on the open sea were not considered sufficient). The *U-38* torpedoed *Persia* without warning and the 200-plus passengers, along with the crew, were left to fend for themselves. Colonel Lord Montague of Beaulieu (colonel of the 2nd Battalion, 7th Hampshire Regiment) was travelling along with other military officers. He was accompanied by his private secretary, Miss Eleanor Thornton, who in 1911 had been modelled as *The Spirit of Ecstasy* which features on Rolls-Royce cars. Whilst he was one of the survivors picked up by the SS *Ningchow* and landed in Malta, she was amongst the 343 who died.

CHAPTER THREE

1916

THE EVACUATION OF THE DARDANELLES

G. Garland from Alton depicted the scene on board the last hospital ship to leave the Dardanelles:

On a grey morning, with the smoke of our burning stores rising in a straight column mingling with the mists that shrouded the heights of the Peninsula, the warship itself appeared suddenly as a spectral form out of the greyness. The little pinnace [a small boat used as a tender to larger vessels] came almost to a dead stop under the white painted hull of the hospital ship, waiting for her last load. It was our fate to watch the closing scenes from the side of the ship while the wards slowly filled with sick and wounded. It was Sunday and while the Padre was cheering the sick and the doctors and nurses dressed the wounded, enemy shells were bursting around us. Our own depleted batteries made feeble reply for it was 'the last day' [Friday, 7 January 1916] and nearly all the guns had gone. All this one could see dimly through the greyness, unaware of the fact they were sending us our last load.

By noon the officers' ward began to fill; two Indian officers, the one moaning and the other victim sadly silent headed the procession. They were victims of the explosions on Chocolate Hill. The little subadar [a rank in the Indian Army which is equivalent to a British lieutenant] in great pain fought with his hands – they were small like a woman's – as they lifted him from stretcher to cot. Following these two came other wounded and sick; one was a commander of an East Lancs battalion – a man who had seen the world. He could not rest in his own bed but wandered through the wards, going from cot to cot, gazing at each patient. To the doctor who questioned him, he said he was quite well, but wounds and sickness had left their mark – he had broken down at the finish. The word 'debility' had been written against his name.

Time passed and the ship's wireless buzzed the signal for departure, the anchor chain rattled, the screws began to turn and the ship steamed slowly ahead carrying her last load from the Peninsula. There were still a few empty cots in the ship but the evacuation was almost at an end. The wounded listened to the slow throb of the engines and the soothing swish of water along the ship's side. The night nurse, a bright capable English girl, went quietly through the wards talking softly to a restless patient here and there. Over one Indian a doctor and nurse in attendance were bending thoughtfully listening, for this one nothing more was to be done. They lowered the brass rods above his cot and left him unconscious, and without a moan he passed away into the unknown land.

When we passed his cot again it was empty. Then the engines became still slower, the swish of the water along the ship's side died away and there was a splash in the dark water, the fire bars at his feet carrying him down, one more body to dot the line of sleeping soldiers marking the track of Red Cross ships to Malta, Alexandria and even to England. The other Indians, knowing nothing of this, had fallen asleep and quiet reigned once more. But all of a sudden the silence was broken with a ringing voice of command 'Get that gun! Get that gun!' It was the voice of 'Debility'. He was fighting his battles over again. Moving quickly but quietly through the ward, the sister was at his side soothing him back to slumber. Then silence again reigned.

At dawn we were once more at anchor and the circle of brown hills that rise above Lemos harbour lay around us. Nine hundred sick and wounded that had been transferred to a troopship in the earlier stages of the evacuation were now re-embarked. Again the anchor chain rattled in the winch and this time the ship headed full speed for Alexandria. A little less than two days brought us in port again where we disembarked our patients and sent them to various hospitals and this ended the voyage of the last wounded from the Peninsula.

HH&AG, 25 March 1916

——————— MILITARY SERVICE ———————

Those who volunteered in the early months of the war were not thought to be sufficient enough numbers for a long war and the government was forced to introduced conscription in January 1916, firstly for single men aged 18–41, then in May for married men. The government pledged not to send teenagers to the front line.

Men could state their case in a local Miliary Service Tribunal to appeal against conscription and often received at least temporary (from a few weeks to six months) exemption. Grounds for appeal included conscientious objection, being medically unfit, performing work of national importance, or a resultant hardship (for instance if the breadwinning family business would be forced to close if the claimant was called up to war service). By the end of June 1916, 748,587 had appealed against conscription and, at the same time, around 770,000 men had enlisted in the armed forces.

Regular reports of the Alton Tribunals for the Urban and Rural District appeared in the local newspaper and at the tribunal held on the morning of 28 February 1916, the assembled town councillors and local recruiting officer heard ten cases. Two were refused, four were granted, two were exempted for three months, and another two were exempted for six months.

In the afternoon, the Rural District Tribunal cases were examined by a panel of councillors and twelve were detailed but no names given. Some with skilled agricultural jobs but poor health were granted exemption, whilst others in good health were refused. One man 'Stated to be almost blind and deaf' and who didn't appear, was exempted as being unfit for service.

MUNITIONS WORKERS

'Here's to the Girls' read a 1916 postcard, praising the female 'munitioneers' who were joining the war effort to help produce the millions of bullets, shells, guns and uniforms that were required to keep the war going. To overcome the early shortages and then maintain production at an increasing rate, the Ministry of Munitions had been established in June 1915 under Lloyd George, who later became prime minister.

34. War Service Badge and poem on a 1916 postcard.

35. Local munitions workers photographed by Aylwards of Alton and Basingstoke.

Alton photographer G.A. Aylward, who had a shop in Market Street, took a picture of local women workers some of whom are wearing a triangular metal badge, which signifies that they are engaged on war service. Newspapers sometimes called these girls who made munitions 'munitionettes', but it was not a word they often used about themselves.

The manufacture of munitions during the war expanded industry and provided employment. As profits grew, frontline soldiers envied the bulging pay packets of civilians in reserved occupations and protected trade unions. The government feared that these high wages would be spent on alcohol, the resulting drunkenness causing inefficiency and accidents. As a result, licensing hours to limit the opening times of public houses were introduced by the Defence of the Realm Act (DORA). Interestingly, the requirement for an afternoon break in opening hours lasted in England until the 1988 Licensing Act came into force.

MESOPOTAMIA

The British occupation of Basra, Turkey's port at the head of the Persian Gulf in November 1914, had been an understandable move to secure the oil wells in Southern Persia (now Iraq) and the vital Abadan oil refinery. The British advance, 46 miles (74km) northwards from Basra to al Qurnah in December and the further advance of 90 miles (144km) up the River Tigris to Kut al Amara in May–June 1915, should have been enough for military purposes, but the push was continued towards Baghdad. Kut was occupied in September 1915, and the advance continued under

Major General Townshend, until the troops were some 500 miles (800km) from their Basra base. Unfortunately, with poor logistical support, training, equipment and command it became very isolated and as a consequence, vulnerable. They fought a battle at Ctesiphon which was only 18 miles (29km) from Baghdad on 22 November 1915, but had to retreat to Kut al Amara. At this small town, situated in a bend of the River Tigris, they were surrounded by Turkish forces and, from 7 December 1915, Townshend's men were besieged. Despite numerous attempts to relieve them, which cost 23,000 casualties, the troops were forced to surrender on 29 April 1916.

This sad episode is regarded as the worst defeat in British military history, and involved many different units, composed of approximately 310 British officers, 2,851 British other ranks, 225 Indian officers and 8,230 Indian other ranks. Included in the above were ten officers and 163 men of the 1st/4th Hampshire Regiment who were in Kut when the siege started.

During the siege, which was notable for constant sniping and shelling, bad weather and a lack of food, 1,025 troops died through enemy action, 721 died from disease, and 2,500 were wounded. Amongst the 13,309 who went into captivity, were all ten officers and 154 men of the Hampshires, whilst nine had died during the siege. There followed a forced march to prison camps in Turkey, during which many of the captured troops died, and two years of captivity with hard labour in poor conditions when thousands more perished.

At the end of the war, the surviving prisoners of war from Turkey were repatriated. All ten of the Hampshire's officers (including Captain Jones, RAMC of Alton) had survived captivity as they had been well looked after, but only forty of the men made it back to Winchester, including Private Knight of Alton. If ever you are visiting St Paul's Cathedral in London, do take time to locate the Kut Memorial to the 5,746 men who died in the Siege of Kut el Amara or afterwards in captivity.

——— SERGEANT PERCIVAL CONRAD CEMERY ———

We record with regret, the death in action in Mesopotamia of Sergeant Percival Conrad Cemery, 1/4 Hants Regt, fourth son of Lieut John B. Cemery, late of Alton. Sergt Cemery was a promising young fellow, 25 years of age, and was in H Company 4th Hants for some years before war broke out. He was a fine soldier, tall, smart looking, and capable, a great favourite with his comrades who we are sure will mourn his loss very deeply.

He comes of a fighting family. His father, an old Scots Guardsman, served through the South African War and has since the war broke out, obtained a commission in the RAMC, to which Corps he belonged before he left the army, and is now acting Quartermaster at Brockenhurst. He has also two other sons serving, one of whom is in France. He has been wounded twice, but happily slightly. Before the war Sergt

Cemery was in the employ of Messrs Kingdon & Co. We are sure the sympathy of the whole town will be shown to Lieutenant & Mrs Cemery in their loss.

HH&AG, 11 March 1916

To show the close connection His Majesty and Lord Kitchener maintained with relatives of men killed, the official notice of Sergeant Cemery's death contained the royal expression of sympathy: 'The King commands me to assure you of the true sympathy of His Majesty and the Queen in your sorrow – Kitchener.'

— BRITISH BATTLESHIP MINED IN THE MEDITERRANEAN —

The Admiralty announces that the battleship HMS *Russell*, flying Admiral Freemantle's flag, struck a mine and sank in the Mediterranean on Thursday. The Admiral, the Captain, 24 Officers and 676 men were saved. 124 officers and men are missing.

HH&AG, 29 April 1916

36. General Post Office, O'Connell Street, Dublin, scene of the Declaration of Independence on Easter Monday, 1916.

HMS *Russell* had entered service in February 1903, took part in the Dardanelles campaign and was involved in the final evacuation. *Russell* was steaming off Malta early on the morning of 27 April 1916 when she struck two mines that had been laid by a German submarine. However, she sank slowly, allowing most of her crew to escape. A total of twenty-seven officers and ninety-eight ratings were lost and among these was Able Seaman H.G. Tune of Alton.

LOCAL MEN AT KUT

The two great events of the past week – the fall of Kut and the rebellion in Dublin – have occasioned considerable anxiety in this town since it was known that several Alton men were included in General Townshend's beleaguered forces, while it transpires that the son of Dr William Curtis is among those who were wounded during the street fighting in the Irish capital.

The fall of Kut came as a severe blow to several Alton families, who had been hoping against hope that the relieving force might succeed in raising the siege before it was too late. Among the Alton men known or believed to be in Kut is Capt C.E.M. Jones, RAMC, son of Dr C.E.M. Jones. Capt Jones belonged to the 4th Hants before the war broke out, and subsequently went to India with his regiment. Since then he has been through the whole of the Mesopotamian campaign. Pte A. Piper, RAMC, is also believed to have been in Kut. He is the son of Mr Alfred Piper of Alton. The last news received from him was in the form of a postcard, which arrived on Christmas morning last, and was written sometime in November. It is understood that the RAMC section attached to the 4th Hants were engaged in bring wounded down the Tigris after one of the earlier battles, and that some of them were unfortunate enough to be left in Kut when the town became infested by the enemy. The greatest sympathy is felt locally for the families affected, and we trust their anxiety will soon be alleviated by news that their loved ones are safe, even if prisoners in the hands of the Turks.

HH&AG, 6 May 1916

37. Able Seaman H.G. Tune was amongst the 125 men lost when HMS *Russell*, a pre-Dreadnought battleship, was sunk by two mines in the Mediterranean on 27 April 1916.

— SECOND LIEUTENANT CURTIS WOUNDED IN DUBLIN —

We regret to learn that Sec. Lieut W.H. Curtis, Notts and Derby Regt, son of
Dr W. Curtis, was among the officers wounded during the Dublin fighting.
He left Alton as recently as Easter Monday and was believed to have arrived in
Dublin on Tuesday last, and to have been wounded on the following day.

HH&AG, 6 May 1916

The Easter Rising began on Easter Monday, 24 April 1916, with the proclama-
tion of an Irish Republic outside the General Post Office in O'Connell Street,
Dublin, and it lasted for six days before order was restored. Some 2,217 rebels
and civilans were wounded during the conflict and 318 died. The British Army
reported 116 casualties with 368 wounded, and the police force lost sixteen of
their number with twenty-nine wounded.

— THE BATTLE OF JUTLAND —

Seven men from Alton and the surrounding area lost their lives at the Battle of
Jutland on 31 May 1916, the great confrontation between the British and German
fleets. First contact was between the rival battlecruiser forces. During that phase
of the battle, the 26,000-ton HMS *Queen Mary* was hit by a salvo of heavy shells.
Within seconds she had blown up, taking with her all but nine of the 1,285 men
on board.

When the battleships of both sides became involved, the 1st Cruiser Squadron
(*Defence*, *Warrior* and *Black Prince*) found themselves briefly exposed to the fire of

38. HMS *Queen Mary* – the battlecruiser
in which Altonians A. Christmas,
F.G. Knight and F. Vince served –
blew up at the Battle of Jutland.

twenty-seven German ships, each about twice the size of the 13,000-ton British cruisers. *Defence* blew up at once with the loss of all 893 on board. The crippled *Warrior* was taken in tow but sank later. *Black Prince* was badly hit and staggered away out of sight of both fleets. Apparently, her crew repaired the damage and she set out to regain her position in the British Fleet. However, by then it was dark and *Black Prince* found instead, the entire German Fleet. There were no survivors out of her crew of 857.

It was during the confusion of that night that the destroyer HMS *Tipperary* was leading her flotilla when she also encountered the German Fleet. Her challenge was answered with a hail of shells at only 800yds range. After blazing for over two hours, the 2,000-ton *Tipperary* sank. By then only thirty-eight out of 200 were still alive and they managed to get away on a life raft, but eight of them died before rescue came.

Both fleets clashed again as the Germans sailed for port. The German ship *Lutzow* was sunk. *Seydlitz* and *Derfflinger* were badly damaged.

The Germans claimed that Jutland was their victory, as they had sunk more capital ships than the British. Admiral Jellicoe claimed that the victory belonged to the British Fleet, which was still a seaworthy entity, whereas the German High Seas Fleet was not. The British did lose more ships (fourteen ships and over 6,000 lives) than the Germans (nine ships and over 2,500 casualties). However, the German Fleet was never again to be in a position to put to sea and challenge the British Navy in the North Sea.

——— PETTY OFFICER STOKER WILLIAM WEEKS ———

William Weeks was born at Holt Lane End, Bentworth on 22 January 1883, the only son of George and Harriett Weeks. He joined the Royal Navy as a stoker when he was 18 and was assigned to HMS *Duke of Wellington* in 1901. He married Lily Frances Binsted on 18 February 1905 at St Lawrence church and they had four children, one of whom died as an infant.

William was serving as a petty officer stoker on HMS *Invincible* when war was declared. The elderly battlecruiser was the flagship of the 3rd Battlecruiser Squadron during the Battle of Jutland and was destroyed by a magazine explosion during the battle. Only six men survived and 1,026 officers and men lost their lives, William amongst them.

The local paper headed its article 'A Tragic Week' when it announced his death and that of two other local men who served on HMS *Invincible* – C.E. White and H. Arnold – the latter hailing from Millcourt, near Froyle while his father lived for some time in Holybourne. 'Special references to the naval battle were made at the evening service at All Saints' church last week and the Dead March was played.'

The Roll of Honour in *HH&AG* included a piece about William Weeks on 10 June 1916, written by 'his sorrowing wife and little ones':

In loving memory of my dear beloved husband, William Weeks, Sto. Petty Officer, who lost his life in action on HMS *Invincible* in Battle of Jutland, 31 May 1916, aged 33.

One of the Best

Rest on, dear one, thy battles are oe'r
Thy willing hands will toil no more,
A devoted husband and father kind
No-one on earth like thee we'll find.

He has gone to his last commission
To that beautiful ship called 'Rest'
And now he is gently sleeping
Safe on his Saviour's breast

HMS *TIPPERARY* AT JUTLAND

HMS *Tipperary* was launched on 5 March 1915. Originally ordered by Chile, *Tipperary* and her three sister ships were bought by the Royal Navy at the outbreak of the Great War. *Tipperary* served in the Harwich Force, arriving there in

39. Ordinary Signalman W.J. Allwork of Alton died when the destroyer HMS *Tipperary* was lost at the Battle of Jutland.

June 1915. Late in that same year, she took charge of a detachment of destroyers from the 2nd Flotilla before being made the leader of the 4th Flotilla in May 1916, a formation which directly supported the Grand Fleet.

On 31 May 1916, *Tipperary* was lost at the Battle of Jutland as her squadron pressed home determined torpedo attacks on the German main battle line as it escaped across the rear of the British Fleet during the confused night action:

> … Captain Wintour and the leading boats of his solitary flotilla were aware of a shadowy line of ships to starboard on a converging course. Whether they were friend or foe it was impossible to tell, and he held on for some minutes with all torpedo tubes trained to starboard. Still they made no sign, and at last, as they were evidently drawing ahead of him and had closed to less than 1,000 yards, he ventured to give the challenge.
>
> Salvoes, accurate and rapid, at point blank followed instantaneously, and in a minute the *Tipperary* burst into flames, almost lost to sight in brilliantly illuminated splashes. Yet she fired both her torpedoes. The four boats of her division did the same, and so did the *Broke*. Some of the rear boats, still uncertain that a mistake was not being made, held their fire till accidentally one of the enemy's beams lit up the rear ship. Then it was plain to see what they had to deal with, and they also attacked. Several of the boats claim to have hits. Explosions were plainly seen; there were gaps in the line of staring searchlights. How many hits were made is uncertain, but one at least of the cruisers received her death blow … All that man could do Captain Wintour had done, but he was now no more. The first salvo had swept away the Tipperary's bridge, on which he stood, and she was left a mass of burning wreckage …'
>
> Extract from Sir Julian S. Corbett, *Naval Operations*, 1923

From a crew of 197 only twelve survived. W.J. Allwork of Alton was amongst those lost.

TRELOAR HOSPITAL

In the early days of the Great War, the hospital was extended by the use of marquees to accommodate war casualties. Later a special ward, then called 'The Fourth Destroyer Flotilla Memorial Ward', was established and dedicated 'To the glorious memory of the officers and men of the Flotilla who lost their lives in the Battle of Jutland.'

In the rebuilding of the hospital after the war, the Naval Wards were established in which memorials were placed recording the names of those who died on the destroyers which were lost. These wards, later known as the Portsmouth Wards,

40. Women employed by the General Post Office as postwomen.

were to provide free treatment for the children of men of the Royal Navy and the Merchant Navy and especially for orphans of those who had given their lives. Following the demolition of the hospital in 2002 the fate of these plaques is unknown.

THE LOSS OF HMS *HAMPSHIRE*

The 11,000-ton armoured cruiser HMS *Hampshire* was launched on 24 September 1903 and joined the Channel Fleet when she was completed on 15 July 1905. Following service in the Mediterranean and on the China station, she was ordered to Scapa Flow, Orkney in 1915 to join the Grand Fleet.

She fought at the Battle of Jutland, returning safely to Scapa Flow on 3 June 1916. Despite bad weather she put to sea two days later, bound for Archangel in North Russia to escort the Secretary of State for War, Lord Kitchener, who was to meet the Czar.

At 7.40 p.m., when *Hampshire* was only 1.5 miles (2.4km) from the shore off Marwick Head, an explosion tore out the centre of the ship, and within fifteen minutes she sank with almost her entire crew of 655 men and seven passengers. Only twelve survived. It was believed that she had struck a mine laid by a German submarine two weeks before.

41. Only twelve men survived the loss of HMS *Hampshire* in June 1916 and amongst over 600
    who died were Lord Kitchener (Secretary of State for War) and Stoker Teddie Rogers of Alton.

Stoker First Class William Rogers of Alton, aged 19 years, was drowned.
His body was one of 124 recovered and identified, and he was buried in Lyness
Royal Naval Cemetery, Orkney on 8 June 1916. There are many unidentified
bodies buried in the same cemetery.

――――――――― LORD KITCHENER MEMORIAL SERVICE ―――――――――

On Tuesday evening at 8 p.m. a memorial service for Lord Kitchener was held
in the parish church. The Vicar [Revd C.R. Stebbing Elvin MA] conducted the
service, which was an adaption of the Burial Service with the special psalms and
hymns as sung in St Paul's Cathedral. Following the lesson was an interval for silent
prayer, during which the Vicar asked for those present to pray for Lord Kitchener
and his staff; for the officers and men of HMS *Hampshire* and for all who gave
their lives in the service in the recent naval battle. There was a large congregation,
the church being well filled. The organist was Miss Batchelor, who played the
'Dead March in Saul' at the conclusion of the service, the choir and congregation
remaining in their places standing. Alton mourned for at least one of her sons,
who shared Kitchener's fate – Teddie Rogers, once a familiar figure to many as
Messrs Smith & Sons newsboy, and lately a Stoker on board HMS *Hampshire*.

HH&AG, 17 June 1916

—————— EDWARD JOHN LASSAM ——————

E.J. Lassam enlisted before the war and went to France as part of the BEF in the summer of 1914. He took part in the Battle of Le Cateau in late August and the subsequent retreat to a reinforced trenched sector. From late 1914 to mid-1915 he spent time in and out of trenches on the Western Front.

On 18 July 1915, the new 3rd British Army was formed and took over a 17-mile sector north of the River Somme. The 1st Hampshires were part of this grouping and on 1 July 1916, together with the other massed regiments, they went into battle close to the site of the village of Beaumont Hamel. At the end of the day, twenty-six officers and 560 other ranks were dead, missing or wounded. Edward Lassam was listed as missing and his body was never found.

42. Edward Lassam (standing) was one of the few Alton men killed on the first day of the Battle of the Somme, 1 July 1916, pictured here with his father, also serving with the Hampshire Regiment.

43. Hampshire regimental badge on a Commonwealth War Graves Commission headstone.

— SECOND LIEUTENANT GEOFFREY CHARLES BOLTON —

General regret is felt throughout Alton at the news of the sad bereavement which has befallen Mr R.C. Bolton, the well-known Alton solicitor, and Mrs Bolton. Their younger son, Sec Lieut Geoffrey Charles Bolton (Sherwood Foresters), having been killed in action on August 1st. The late Lieut Bolton was formerly on the staff of the London & South Western Railway, and had a number of friends in Alton. He was a server at All Saints Church where on Thursday evening, the 'Vespers of the Dead' were said in his memory. He was only 18 years of age at the time of his death, but was a promising young officer whose untimely end is sincerely regretted by all those who knew him. The greatest sympathy is felt and expressed with Mr & Mrs Bolton in their hour of sorrow.

HH&AG, 12 August 1916

WORKING THE LAND

The formation of the Women's Land Army, the introduction of rationing and new ways of guarding merchant ships, prevented the total starvation of the British people. However, some foods were still in short supply and there were never enough agricultural workers, especially at harvest time. On such occasions, soldiers on leave or convalescence were encouraged to help on local fields. In some places

44. Belgian refugees helping on a local farm photographed by H.A. Aylward of Alton and Basingstoke.

45. Soldier helping with the harvest in the Alton–Basingstoke area.

troops in training or on garrison duty were allocated to neighbouring farms until the hay and corn had been cut and gathered in. Locally, Belgian refugees were drafted in to help and there was also a detachment of German prisoners of war from a large prison camp at Dorchester in Dorset, who were based at the former paper mill, by King's Pond in Alton, and also worked on local farms.

- CEMETERIES AT THE FORMER POTIJZE CHATEAU, NEAR YPRES -

The former chateau grounds at Potijze, just north-east of Ypres, are now the site of three small war cemeteries hidden behind a line of modern houses alongside the road and backing on to farmland. They contain over 850 Commonwealth burials from the Great War. For most of the war, the village of Potijze was held by the Commonwealth forces but it stood directly behind the Allied trenches and was well within range of the German guns. It was here that soldiers entered the communication and support trenches that led to the front line. Potijze was never quiet and, on the evening of Tuesday, 8 August 1916, the 1st and 2nd Battalions of the Hampshire Regiment, having spent ten days in local trenches, were preparing to leave. The Germans staged a surprise attack using poison gas and both units were caught unawares. Although no ground was lost, the 1st Battalion had nearly seventy casualties: fourteen men were killed, died of gas or were reported missing, nearly forty others suffered the effects of being gassed and a number more were wounded. The 2nd Battalion suffered over 240

46. Graves of forty-six men from the 1st and 2nd Battalions of the Hampshire Regiment, including Lance Corporal Charles Doe of Alton, who were killed near Ypres following a German gas attack on 8 August 1916.

casualties, about half of whom were killed. Included amongst these was Lance Corporal Charles Doe from Alton and he lies buried in one of these three small cemeteries with forty-five of his comrades. The headstones are arranged in two lines and stand side by side almost touching, indicating that the men died together.

LIEUTENANT WRIGHT KILLED IN ACTION

It is with deep regret that we have to record the death of Second Lieutenant Arthur Wright, of the Royal Warwickshire Regiment, who was a well-known figure in the town and held in high esteem as a former master at Eggar's Grammar School. His parents received the following letter from Captain E.D. Baskin:

'Dear Mrs Wright, It is with the deepest sympathy that I have to inform you that your son was killed this morning. As I have just lost my only brother, I can well understand what a heavy blow this will be and I feel most deeply for you in your loss. We, too, shall greatly miss him. At two o'clock this morning, he was on duty with some guns on an advanced point, when a large shell landed quite close to him and a big splinter went right through his heart, killing him instantly.'

Second Lieutenant Wright was 26. He had a brilliant scholastic career. As a boy, he first attended the People's College, Warrington, and later transferred to the Grammar School of that town. With a view to entering the teaching profession, he graduated at the Manchester University, obtaining his BA and MA. For a short time he occupied the position of classics master at Hutton Grammar School, near Preston, and later became second master at Eggar's Grammar School, Alton.

He left here [Alton] in March 1915, having obtained a commission as Second Lieutenant in the Royal Warwicks. He was later placed in charge of the Depot of the Royal Warwicks, and then transferred for special work in Egypt, where he was soon placed in charge of an important piece of work on the east of Suez. He then specialised in machine-gun work and was transferred to the Machine Gun Company. It may be mentioned that in his machine-gun examinations, he obtained 97% of the possible marks. In August 1916 he was sent to France, and took part in the preliminary movements of the attack on 15 September in which he met his death.

During his time at the Grammar School here he proved himself to be a devoted and loyal colleague who placed the good of the school first. The qualities which he displayed in his work there must have been of the highest value in the greater work to which he was called. His death is deeply regretted by the staff and pupils, who had a deep affection for him, and who held him in grateful remembrance for his work there. It has already been suggested that a small fund should be raised with which to extend the school library and thus make a permanent memorial in the school to one who gave up all for his country. He proved himself to be a true and loyal Christian, and was most regular in his attendance at the Parish Church. He also took an active part in the work of the Alton Volunteer Training Corps and was a Section Commander of that organisation.

HH&AG, 20 September 1916

——— PRIVATE H.J. WHITE KILLED IN ACTION ———

Information has been received that Pte H.J. White, Somerset Light Infantry, son of Mr & Mrs H. White of Nursery Cottages, Alton was killed in action on 28 August. Deceased was 25 years of age [and] had served in India and then in France, where he was wounded in the right hand a few months ago. He returned to the fighting line after treatment at a base hospital in Boulogne. He came home to Alton on service leave last Easter. Much sympathy has been evinced with his bereaved parents.

HH&AG, 27 September 1916

PRIVATE V.W. BRIER

News has been received of the death from wounds at a casualty station in France, on 18 September, of Pte Victor William Brier, East Surrey Regiment (the adopted son of Mr Henry Brier of No. 21 Amery Street, Alton). The deceased, who was 19 years of age, was well known in Alton where he was active as a Sergeant in the Church Lads' Brigade associated with the parish of All Saints'. He was much liked by his comrades, respected by his employers (Messrs Kingdon & Co) who have heard with much regret of his early death in the cause of his country.

HH&AG, 4 October 1916

PRISONERS OF WAR

Pte E. Powell, a married man of the 1st Hampshire Regiment and a prisoner of war in Germany, has recently written to his mother, Mrs Sturgeon of No. 38 Church Street, Alton, to thank those who have sent comforts out to him. He states, however, that he and his fellow prisoners are in very urgent need of waistcoats, braces and handkerchiefs. Mrs Sturgeon will be very pleased to send any such gifts which friends of the men may wish to provide. Pte E. Powell will be remembered by many as a former member of the Alton Fire Brigade.

His brother, Pte F. Powell, also a prisoner of war, writes that he and his companions in misfortune are being better treated and receiving their parcels more regularly than was formerly the case.

HH&AG, 18 November 1916

47. Transporting British prisoners of war; from a postcard sent by a German soldier to his family in Berlin.

The men, along with A. Gilliam, who was also of the Hampshire Regiment (and Privates G. Barnet, R. Norris and W.G. Parrack of the RMLI), had been taken prisoner following the fall of Antwerp on 10 October 1914. This resulted in a retreat westwards to the coast of the Anglo-Belgian forces, although some 2,000 British troops and 20,000 Belgians were cut off by the Germans and compelled to escape into neutral Dutch territory, where they had to lay down their arms. The troops were interned in Holland for the duration of the war.

LEADING SEAMAN HENRY HURLOCK

HM Submarine *E30* was mined off Orford Ness, Suffolk in the North Sea on 22 December 1916. There were no survivors from her crew of thirty-one, which included Leading Seaman Henry Hurlock DSM of Alton. He joined the Royal Navy in 1907 and was awarded the Distinguished Service Medal following an engagement at Heligoland Bight on 28 August 1914 (as reported in the *London Gazette*, 20 October 1914).

THE ALTON–BASINGSTOKE RAILWAY

At the outbreak of hostilities all Britain's railways were put under government control and day-to-day management was entrusted to the Rail Executive Committee. In October 1916 they wrote to the railway companies asking for second-hand materials or whether they had any sections of line which could be closed so that the rails might be recovered and sold to the War Department. Unable to get the desired response, additional pressure was applied in early December with a demand for fare increases, reduced passenger services and the closure of branch lines. Some 200 miles (320km) of materials were wanted and each railway company was given a figure based on the size of their system. The London and South Western Railway 'target' was set at 12 miles (*c.* 19km) and it was decided that this could be met by the closure of the Alton to Basingstoke line. Local communities were only given a week's notice of the closure and the last train ran on Saturday, 30 December 1916, until further notice. This was accepted by Alton as being necessary for the war effort and the rails were lifted and transported to France.

Early 1917 would see the movement of both men and supplies transformed by the establishment of the Royal Engineers Light Railways companies. They constructed a link between existing French railways on the Western Front to the front lines of the conflict, easing the delays in equipment and sustenance, which had been common until this point, and allowing men to make the final leg of their journey to the front by train.

CHAPTER FOUR

1917

---------------- PRIVATE FREDERICK DICKER ----------------

We regret to announce the death in action on 28 January of Pte Frederick
W. Dicker of the Hampshire Regiment. The deceased was the only son of
Mr & Mrs F. Dicker of Amery Hill and great sympathy is felt for them in their
bereavement. Pte Dicker was formerly in the employ of Mr H. Adlam of Alton.
He joined the colours in November 1915 and was sent to India a few months
later and met his death during the recent fighting in Mesopotamia.

HH&AG, 16 February 1917

48. Silk postcard with flowers in the national colours of the Allies – including the USA who
entered the Great War on 6 April 1917.

PRIVATE P. BEAGLEY

We regret to announce the death of Pte P. Beagley of the Hampshire Regiment who was killed in action on 30 January in France. He joined nearly two years ago and was recently transferred to the Hampshire Regiment. Previous to joining up he was for some time with Mr Morris, Butcher. He was not quite 21 years of age at the time of his death. His parents, who reside at No. 43 Victoria Road [Alton], have three other sons serving. The eldest, who belongs to the Northumberland Fusiliers, was wounded in France last May. He has been in hospital in Woolwich ever since, and is still unable to walk by himself. One other son is at the Gulf and another is Drummer of a regiment at Bournemouth.

HH&AG, 16 February 1917

THE DOVER PATROL

From time to time during the Great War, German destroyers attempted to attack British cross-Channel traffic and its defence was borne by the destroyers of the Dover Patrol. HMS *Viking*, launched in 1909, was one of twelve tribal class destroyers, part of the 6th Destroyer Flotilla, and although she survived the war, *Viking* was damaged on a number of occasions. Stoker First Class Jack Harding was killed following one of these actions on 16 November 1914.

Another of the 6th Destroyer Flotilla was the 928-ton *Paragon* launched by Thornycroft at Southampton on 21 March 1913. On the night of 17/18 March 1917, she challenged and fired at an unidentified warship. Struck in reply by a torpedo, she sank in eight minutes. There were only two survivors from a crew of seventy-five. Leading Seaman Henry Allwork from Alton was lost – another sad blow for his family, as his brother had died the year before in HMS *Tipperary* at the Battle of Jutland.

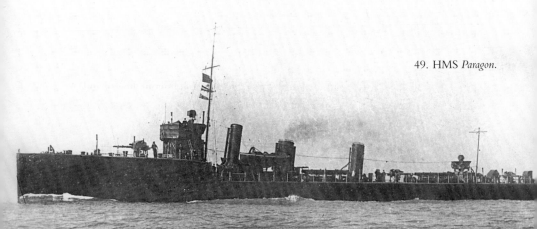

49. HMS *Paragon*.

50. H.W. (seated) and W.J. Allwork in Royal Navy
uniform. The latter died in HMS *Tipperary*
in the Battle of Jutland, 1916, whilst his older
brother was drowned when HMS *Paragon* sank in
March 1917.

DIED AT KUT

Mr G. Morgan of No. 33 Turk Street has received information that his son
Private James Morgan of the Hampshire Regiment, who was taken prisoner
at Kut, has died of disease. Deceased who had been employed at the Borovere
Laundry, Alton joined up in August 1914 when he was 19 years of age.

He was wounded in December 1915 and four months later was taken prisoner. His parents have received seven postcards from him, the last in November
[1916] when he said that he was quite well and that they need not worry.
They had sent several parcels, but had received no acknowledgement.

HH&AG, 23 March 1917

CALVARY AND WAR MEMORIAL

On Good Friday, Alton was deeply and reverently interested in the impressive ceremony connected with the unveiling of the Calvary and War Memorial, which has
been erected by the generous subscriptions of parishioners, in front of All Saints'
church. In design it is a chaste and beautiful memorial, which in the striking position it occupies will help the man in the street to realise what the men of Alton
have done and are still doing in the great struggle to preserve honour, liberty and
Christianity. It is hoped that photographic souvenirs of this shrine will find their
way across the seas to the men of Alton, who will thus feel they are remembered in
prayerful thankfulness by those whom they have left behind.

HH&AG, 13 April 1917

——— ALTON INSTITUTE AND CURTIS MUSEUM ———

Sir, It is with very great regret that the Committee has to announce the temporary closing of the premises on 21 April as they are needed by the Red Cross Hospital for additional accommodation. We are sure the members will gladly suffer any inconvenience and loss to themselves for so good a cause; and when we are able to resume our occupancy we shall be pleased to credit them with the unexpired time due to those who have paid their subscriptions for the year ending 30 September 1917.

Charles Archer, Hon. Secretary & Treasurer

HH&AG, 13 April 1917

——— PRIVATE W.D. RANDALL ———

Randall – on 15 April 1917, died of wounds received in the Battle of Vimy Ridge. Pte Randall, Overseas Batt. (Canadian). Son of Mr & Mrs Frank Randall, Victoria Road, Alton, aged 27.

Roll of Honour, *HH&AG*, 20 April 1917

51. A woman recruited to the Women's Land Army.

The eldest and dearly beloved brother of Annie Simmons, Beech Mount, Beech, W.D. Randall was buried in Wimereux, a small town 5km north of Boulogne, which was the headquarters of Queen Mary's Army Auxiliary Corps. From October 1914 onwards, Boulogne and Wimereux formed an important hospital centre and, until June 1918, the medical units at Wimereux used the local cemetery for burials.

───────────── DEATH OF ANOTHER ALTONIAN ─────────────

It is with deep regret that we have to announce the death from wounds in action of Sergt G. Mills of the Hampshire Regiment and of Vicarage Road, Alton. Last Saturday his friends received information that he had been dangerously wounded and on the following morning came the sad intelligence that he had succumbed to his wounds. Deceased in civil life was a town postman attached to the Alton Post Office in which he commenced his official career as a telegraph boy. He was highly respected and in his youth an active member of the Church Lads' Brigade connected with All Saints'. He had previously been twice wounded at Suvla Bay, Gallipoli; he recovered from his wounds, was afterwards attacked with fever and sent to England. He spent some time in hospitals at Birmingham and Warminster and on his recovery went to the Gosport depot and was transferred to Reading to undergo a course of instruction in Trench work. Proceeding to Salonica he was attached to a Labour Battalion.

Just recently his parents (Mr & Mrs G. Mills, No. 9 Tanhouse Lane) received a letter from him in which he said he was in the pink of condition. 'I am,' he wrote, 'in a very quiet spot; there is absolutely no life at all excepting hundreds of tortoises crawling about. My little dugout is situated in a wood something like Great Wood, but the trees are not so large. So you see I am living in a miniature zoo.'

Deceased, who was 32 years of age, leaves a widow for whom the deepest sympathy is felt. His father is a member of the Alton Urban Tribunal and one of the oldest members of the Alton Fire Brigade. Another son is serving in the Navy.

The late Sergt Mills, during a stay in hospital in England, wrote the following description of his experiences:

'Soon after the war broke out, I, like many others, joined the Army, and was sent to Ireland where I was stationed first at Mullingar and later at the Curragh, my regiment being moved at the end of a few months training to Basingstoke. [This account seems to correspond with the movements of the 10th Hampshire Regiment.] At the end of six weeks we received orders to go abroad. Naturally we all thought we were destined for France, but when we were served out with [pith] helmets and drill khaki, we knew we should not go there and were all rather disappointed. Very shortly after, however, we made a move and after a long and tedious journey we found ourselves at the port [Liverpool] from which we sailed on 7 July 1915. The voyage was a very pleasant one as regards weather, but we were terribly crowded. Before reaching Gibraltar a fresh escort picked us up, to protect us from attack by the German submarines in the Mediterranean. As we stayed there a short time we had a good opportunity to admire the Rock of 'Gib' which was a wonderful sight.

Coaling at Malta on 14 July, we reached Alexandria two days later, where we were to stay for three days. Everyone was looking forward to this, for during the voyage we had been given lectures on the interesting sights there, and instructions on how to make the most of our time on shore. Imagine our disappointment on arriving there to be told that no one was to go on shore. For three interminable days we lay in the harbour, gazing with longing eyes at the lovely city, which some of us were destined to visit later under very different circumstances. Even now we did not know to where we were going but we were not to remain in ignorance much longer, for leaving Alexandria we landed two days later on a small island off the coast of Greece, where we found the climate most trying.

A few days later we embarked once more and this time we knew we were for Gallipoli and some 'Turkish Delight'. Anzac [Cove] was reached and the fun began when we commenced to land in the darkness. It was a very trying bit of work, for we had to get into small boats tied together in strings of five or six which were towed ashore by motor boats during which proceedings we were tossed about like corks on the water, and I thought of our crossing from Ireland. Luckily our casualties were very slight, only one man being shot.

From the beach we could see some high mountains, up which we had to climb. Whilst attempting this we came under heavy fire from the Turks, who had by that time discovered us, and kept up an incessant and terrific bombardment with their big guns. On the way I discovered some wire entanglements which stuck into me in a most unpleasant fashion, whilst in 'Shrapnel Gully' a bullet hit me in the left side, fortunately not doing any serious damage, and as it was quite impossible for me to be taken out of the range of fire, I was bandaged up and put in a large dugout where the doctors worked.

While taking part in an attack on the 21st [August], when we captured Hill 971, I had two remarkable escapes, a shell pitching right at my feet but failing to explode, and a sniper's bullet passing through the bottom of my nose, smashing my rifle and just grazing my hand.

The heat was terrible and the flies were beyond description. Added to this, difficulties of transport made it almost impossible to keep us supplied with food. There were no roads, the country was mountainous and it was impossible to get out of the range of the enemy's guns, our food had to be brought up by Indians on pack mules and our rations consisted of biscuits, jam and flies.

52. A detachment of the Royal Naval Division going 'over the top' in an action in Gallipoli.

When the order came to withdraw I was detailed to assist a man who was wounded in the leg. As I could not carry him, I stayed with him till dark and then got him down the hillside by dragging [him] along the rough ground by his uninjured leg, thinking every man who overtook us was a Turk. It was a terrible experience, but I am glad to say we reached the beach in safety and he is now recovering from his wound.

I saw many brave deeds done out there, both by men assisting their wounded comrades, and by our machine gun men, many of whom have received the DCM for continuing to fire their guns until the Turks were almost upon them.

After about five weeks of this life, my comrades in the reinforcements which had arrived, did not recognise me, for I had not had a wash for the whole of the time and had grown a lovely beard. I was rather hurt by their remarks, but on seeing myself in a mirror, I considered they were quite justified.

Soon after this I fell ill with enteric fever and dysentery and was sent to hospital on Mudros, returning to England in December to a convalescent camp from where I went to my depot. There I contracted tonsillitis and after having my tonsils removed, I came to Longleat on 11 July 1916.'

HH&AG, 11 May 1917

G.F. TARRANT

With impressive ceremonial and in the presence of a large gathering, the remains of Driver G.F.Tarrant of French's Court in the High Street [located on the present site of Marks and Spencer] who died of pneumonia in the

53. George Tarrant was buried in Alton Cemetery on 14 May 1917.

Isolation Hospital, Aldershot were interred in Alton Cemetery on Monday afternoon [14 May 1917].

The deceased soldier, aged 45, had seen 21 years' service for which he held two medals and King Edward's Coronation medal. He went through the South African campaign and had retired but when war broke out he had volunteered again. He was serving with the 580th Company, Army Service Corps in Aldershot, a unit responsible for local transport services when he became ill and died.

He was a member of the Men's Society at All Saints' and was much respected in Alton where he left a wife and two children for whom great sympathy is felt. The deceased was highly spoken of by his Commanding Officer and the men of his Company.

The coffin, draped with the Union Jack and covered with floral tributes, was conveyed on a gun carriage from Aldershot accompanied by 18 non-commissioned officers and men, six of whom acted as bearers. At Aldershot there was an impressive procession to the railway station headed by the members of the RAOB Lodge [Royal Antediluvian Order of Buffaloes] of which [the] deceased was a member. The funeral procession was formed at the residence of the deceased, and proceeded to All Saints' Church where the service was conducted by the Revd C. Bond.

The carriages conveying the mourners were preceded to the cemetery by mounted men with a detachment of Army Transport men bringing up the rear. At the cemetery the coffin was removed from the gun carriage and conveyed by six of his comrades to the graveside where the committal was read. A trumpeter sounded the 'Last Post', the men lined up at the graveside and sprinkled laurel leaves on the coffin as they departed.

HH&AG, 19 May 1917

JOHN ENGLISH LOTT

John English Lott was born to John and Marion Lott on 17 April 1875, at Ashen House in Suffolk. He was tutored at home before being sent to Framlingham College, aged 13, and later worked in London as a bank clerk.

54. John English Lott joined the army as a private after serving as a Brother at Alton Abbey.

When he was 21, John heard a sermon preached in a city church by an enthusiastic young priest, Father Hopkins. He was inspired to join the Order of Saint Paul and came to Alton Abbey around 1897–98 to help turn around the fortunes of their farm. In 1904, he was sent to Greenwich as prior to sort out the financial problems of the London branch of the order's work, but returned to Alton later that year and was appointed prior there in early 1905, a position he held for five years. During this time the abbey church was built.

Brother John was keen to help serving seamen and worked at the Community House in Barry, South Wales, as well as travelling to the port of Antwerp to provide aid and support. He returned to the UK in 1912 when he was 'lent' to the Cardiff branch of the National Sailors' and Firemen's Union. The following year he moved to Greenwich to assist in the educational aspect of assisting merchant sailors to improve conditions as well as more political work advocating better conditions for seamen.

55. The headstone of Second Lieutenant J.E. Lott MC in La Chapelette Cemetery, Péronne, Somme, France.

With the outbreak of war, the Brethren were allowed to join the armed forces and John joined the Universities' and Public Schools' Battalion of the Royal Fusiliers and was promoted to lance corporal. On his leave days he spent time at Greenwich and visited Alton Abbey, and letters to the abbey were reprinted in their newsletter. On August 1916 the newletter reported that he was, '… writing from a dugout 17ft [5m] below the surface, shells whistling overhead and several had fallen nearby, but beyond being smothered in dirt, he and his comrades in the dugout had been untouched.' In September 1916, John met up with his younger brother, Harry (1877–1975), who was serving as a captain in the Royal Engineers.

A newsletter report of January 1917 mentions John's promotion to officer and a transfer to the Royal Engineers. The following month, while on home leave, he visited Greenwich Priory and was described as follows: 'He is one of those with whom Army life agrees. He looked wonderfully fit and was in excellent spirits.'

John was wounded on 7 May 1917 and died in hospital on 20 May. He was buried in a small cemetery at La Chapelette, Péronne on Wednesday, 23 May.

The London Gazette of 26 July 1917 carried the following citation for the award of a Military Cross to John Lott:

> For conspicuous gallantry and devotion to duty. A party went out to recover the body of a comrade and came under heavy fire which wounded all members of the party. This officer went to their assistance, helped to dress their wounds and carried them to a place of safety. This was carried out under continuous shell fire.

John is commemorated in six places – the cemetery in Péronne; on the war memorial above the south porch entrance to Great Wenham church in Suffolk, as well as on an individual brass plaque in the church; on the war memorial in Framlingham College Chapel; on a ledger stone in Alton Abbey Cemetery; on the plaque on the Cairn, High Street, Alton; and on the Roll of Honour in St Lawrence church, Alton.

SERGEANT WILLIAM MARLOW

Sergeant William Marlow of The King's Royal Rifles, whose death is recorded from wounds received in action, was a well-known football player, having been Captain of the Alton Excelsior team which had won so many notable victories. He was 29 and prior to joining up had worked for Mr D.J. Kemp, Builder. He was a good sportsman, very popular and much respected in Alton. News of his death has been received with deep regret by his mother [Mrs Osgood] and relatives at No. 23 Butts Road and much sympathy has been expressed.

He was wounded on 14 May and the Chaplin wrote to his mother to inform her that his injuries were not regarded as serious 'as he enjoyed a good tea and was very cheery. He asked me to give you his love and to say he is going on alright, and on his way home. Keep your pecker up and thank God that his life has been spared and that he will be out of more fighting. We are doing gloriously.' He died on 25 May 1917.

HH&AG, 8 June 1917

———— MARKING THE GRAVES OF THE FALLEN ————

The neat, well-organised rows of white Portland Stone headstones that characterise the cemeteries which school parties visit on trips to the Somme or Flanders, are a more modern manifestation of the human cost of the Great War. The great battles of the past were rarely marked by such poignant burial places. There is nothing at Waterloo, for example, and whilst there might be a few memorials in English cathedrals and country churches relating to a lost son of the aristocracy in small forgotten wars, ordinary soldiers who died seem to have been neglected.

The origins of the Commonwealth War Graves Commission (CWGC) are outlined in *The Unending Vigil* by Philip Longworth. What began as an effort by the Red Cross to record the graves of soldiers killed during the fighting, became an organisation that created cemeteries, provided permanent care for the graves

56. Wooden grave markers in Bucquoy Road Cemetery, near Arras, France.

and commemoration of the missing. That 1.1 million men and women lost their lives in the service of the British Empire over all parts of the globe during the Great War, gives a sense of scale to the task.

Therefore burials that took place after battles were organised into cemeteries, the original grave markers being replaced by wooden crosses, which themselves were replaced in due course by the white headstones.

One of the decisions that had to be made early on in the war concerned the repatriation of remains and private memorials. It was eventually agreed that neither should be allowed, in an effort to avoid class distinction that would conflict with the feeling of 'brotherhood' that had developed between all ranks serving at the front. Perhaps this is easier to appreciate a century later, but at the time it caused great upset.

It was decided that cemeteries would be marked by rows of standard headstones, of a uniform height and width, the graves being levelled to a flat surface and planted with turf and flowers. The rows would also maintain a military idea, giving the appearance of men on parade. The uniform headstones would convey the notion of equality, but in order to avoid them being too dull and repetitive the design on them should be varied.

Each headstone bears the regimental badge, name, rank, regiment, date of death, and if wanted, a short inscription supplied by the next of kin. Relatives were allowed to choose and pay for an inscription or text of up to sixty-six letters and spaces.

The first cemetery was finished in 1920 and, by 1927 (the tenth anniversary of the organisation that became the CWGC), over 500 cemeteries on the Western Front were completed.

57. Women employed in the manufacture of shells.

In the summer of 2013, the CWGC buried two men who were killed in 1917, following their discovery by a French farmer whilst ploughing his fields. Luckily they could be identified by items found with their remains and the ceremony provided an opportunity for relatives to honour family members posted as missing all those years ago. This is not an isolated incident as engineering works for roads and buildings across the former battlefields of the Western Front often reveal human remains and military material, including unexploded shells and bullets.

One wonders if, in the years following the Great War, many Alton families managed to visit the grave of a loved one or a memorial bearing their name. In the past ten years an awareness of remembrance seems to have been reawakened, suggested by some as a response to the involvement of the armed forces in more recent conflicts in the Middle East and the inevitable loss of life that has resulted.

THE FARM TRACTOR IN ALTON DISTRICT

Very few parts of the country are being so actively developed by the agrimotors as is East Hampshire. The Hampshire War Agricultural Committee has a growing number of tractors under its control, which, under the supervision of its qualified instructors, are being sent from farm to farm. This organisation is particularly active and many acres of land which have lain fallow for years are being converted to arable. Farmers who do not readily fall in line with this modern development are having their farms taken from them by the committee, while labour being short, owing to the neglect of agriculture in the past, farming men from Devon, and soldiers released for work on the land are being employed.

HH&AG, 8 June 1917

SALVATION ARMY FLAG DAY

Tomorrow [Saturday] in Alton and throughout the country is War Flag Day on behalf of the Salvation Army who cater for 3,000 soldiers weekly. It is hoped that the inhabitants of Alton will generously support the good work of the Army who send thousands of parcels every fortnight to our interned men. At the present time the cost of the parcels works out at £4,500 per year, and General Booth is appealing on 9 June for assistance in carrying on this needful agency, and for other services benefiting the men of His Majesty's Forces.

The Salvation Army has erected 153 refreshment and recreation huts in the military camps in Great Britain, France and other countries at a cost of £70,000. Seventy-seven hostels and naval and military homes with 4,000 beds, costing over £80,000, are in operation, whilst extensions amounting to £20,000 are in progress. Thirty motor ambulance cars have been supplied for the war zones in France, Russia and Egypt at an expense of £16,000. Thirty thousand wives and relatives of service men have been entertained at tea and social gatherings. Forty-one thousand food parcels and articles of clothing have been sent to prisoners of war and the troops.

HH&AG, 8 June 1917

————— WILLIAM THOMAS KENWARD —————

Born in 1881 in Oxted, Surrey, William Kenward was working as a grocer's assistant in 1901 and four years later married Annie Read. The date they came to Alton is not recorded and, although their children were born in 1912 and 1914, it was not until 1 July 1917 that they were both baptised at All Saints' church in Alton.

Their father was killed just three weeks later near Passchendaele to the East of Ypres. William is the only soldier from Alton who has a grave in the huge Tyne Cot Cemetery where 11,956 Commonwealth servicemen of the Great War are buried. Of these, 8,369 of the burials are unidentified but there are special memorials to more than eighty casualties known or believed to be buried among them.

If you only visit one CWGC cemetery make it this one. It was designed to represent an English country churchyard and, with its Portland Stone headstones and flint walls, it bears a resemblance to many Hampshire village cemeteries.

58. William Kenward is the only Alton man to be buried in the Tyne Cot Cemetery at Zonnebeke in Flanders, one of the casualties of the Third Battle of Ypres, often referred to as Passchendaele. The stone wall surrounding the cemetery is the Memorial to the Missing and includes almost 35,000 names.

——————— THE ROYAL DEFENCE CORPS ———————

The Royal Defence Corps (RDC) was formed in August 1917 and evolved from the 'National Reserve', which originated at the beginning of the war. Early on they wore the 'GR' armband, 'Georgius Rex', which was the butt of much humour and led to them being called 'the gorgeous wrecks' – mainly because many were over-age ex-soldiers. They primarily performed home defence duty and also guarded various internment camps.

59. Harry Gill of the Royal Defence Corps, the Great War equivalent of the Home Guard in the Second World War, was buried in Alton Cemetery early in 1917.

——————— PRIVATE RICHARD PARRACK ———————

We regret to announce that Pte Richard Parrack, of No. 14 Tower Street, Alton, who was reported wounded and missing since 17 October 1916, has now been officially reported killed on that date. Deceased, who was 35 years of age, leaves a widow and three children. He was an old soldier of the Hampshire Regiment, was in the Reserve, and was called up for service when the war broke out. He went to the Dardanelles, to Egypt and from thence to France. He had not been home for the past two years. As a regular soldier he had many years of meritorious service to his credit. He was awarded the African medal (with two bars) for service in Somaliland (East Africa) and had also served several years in India. By trade he was a painter and worked for the late Mr J. Burfoot of The Butts, Alton.

His mother, who lives at No. 29 Church Street, Alton, has also received information that her son Charles, who is a Private with the Canadian forces, has been wounded in the head in France. Four other brothers are also serving.

HH&AG, 24 August 1917

—————————— PRIVATE WILLIAM PORCH ——————————

Mrs Porch, No. 1 Heap Street, Besses o' the Barn, Manchester (formerly of Alton) has received official notification that her husband, Pte William Porch, aged 25, who had been employed at Crowley's Brewery for the past 9 years, had been killed in Salonica on 1 August 1917. He was a Londoner by birth, but at the outbreak of war he joined the Hampshire Regiment. He was a blacksmith's labourer for the Waterdale Bleaching Co., Prestwich. He had previously been in the Navy and two brothers are still serving there with another in the Army. He was wounded in France and invalided to the Church Lane Hospital at Whitefield, and was, on leaving the institution, married to Mrs Porch, who has been left with two children. Recently she received a letter from him saying he was well, but wished the war was over. He was on the *Rolls of Honour* of the Roman Catholic Church, Prestwich, and Strand Church. Much sympathy is felt for the bereaved widow and his mother, who lives at No. 35 Church Street, Alton.

HH&AG, 24 August 1917

—————————— SERGEANT JAMES LILLYWHITE ——————————

The text of a black-edged memorial card produced by James Lillywhite's wife reads:

For King and Country
In Loving Memory
Of my Dear Beloved husband
Sergt James Lillywhite,
1/9th Hants Regiment
Who died at the Station Hospital, Ferozepore, India on
September 1st 1917
Aged 40 years
Under the soil of a Foreign Land,
My Soldier Husband is laid,
No loved ones stood around
To hear his last farewell,
No words of comfort could he leave,
To those he loved so well.
Step on dear one and take thy rest;
For God has called thee when He thought best;
Our loss is great but thine is gain,
In heaven we hope to meet again.

PRIVATE WILLIAM DEADMAN

The funeral of Private William Deadman (late of the Hussars) who died on Tuesday 16 October at the home of his parents, Mr & Mrs Deadman, Beulah, Beech, took place on Friday [19 October 1917].

The military authorities sent a gun carriage drawn by six black horses and in charge of a mounted Sergeant. The coffin was wrapped in the Union Jack and the service at the parish church and graveside was conducted by Revd P. Morgan Watkins.

William Deadman had served over eight years in the Hussars and was invalided home from India last March. He has a brother serving in the Army and another in the Navy.

HH&AG, 26 October 1917

ALTONIAN'S DEATH IN BAGHDAD

Very general sympathy has been shown to Mr & Mrs A. Piper, Market Street, Alton who have just received the sad intelligence that their only son, Private A.S. Piper, RAMC, attached Hants Regt, who was taken prisoner at Kut in November 1915, died in Baghdad Hospital on or about 4 June 1916. For a year and a half Mr & Mrs Piper have been without direct news. From many sources information was obtained which led them to entertain the firm hope that their son was still alive. The last information received was contained in a postcard dated 3 June 1916, the day before, it is curious to note, which is given as the probable date of his death, in which the deceased soldier said he was quite safe and asking his parents not to worry.

Recently Sergt Rolfe, of Alton, a school chum wrote home saying he had made enquiries, and 'up to the present they continue to say he is alive, as they have received no notice whatever about him', and suggesting that he might be in camp and unable to write. Private Piper was among the first of the Territorials who left Salisbury Plain for India on 9 October 1914. He was 24 years of age at the time of his sad death, which is deeply deplored by his many friends.

HH&AG, 7 December 1917

FIVE SONS SERVING

Mrs Gilliam of Bow Street, Alton has five sons serving: Pte E. Gilliam (missing since 21 January 1916); Pte A. Gilliam, Hants Regt (prisoner of war since the battle of Mons); Lce-Corpl W. Gilliam and Drummer Fred Gilliam, now serving with the Hants Regt in Egypt; and Sergt Walter Gilliam, who has joined the American forces.

HH&AG, 7 December 1917

——— ANOTHER ALTONIAN KILLED IN PALESTINE ———

Mrs Gilliam of Bow Street, Alton has this week received the sad news of the death of her youngest son, Drummer Fred Gilliam, who was killed in action on 22 November. Only recently she received a letter from him saying he was quite all right; they passed through Gaza on 7 November and he was on outpost duty on a hill from which he could just get a glimpse of Jerusalem, which as our readers know, has since been taken. Another son is also serving in Egypt.

HH&AG, 14 December 1917

——— PRIVATE WALTER EMERY KILLED IN ACTION ———

News has been received that Pte Walter F. Emery was killed in action during November between Gaza and Jerusalem, with the Egyptian Expeditionary Force. Pte Walter Francis Emery was a son of James Emery of *The Welcome*, High Street, Alton, where he was well known and greatly respected. He was 31 years of age and leaves a widow and one child whom he had not seen.

HH&AG, 14 December 1917

Walter had been born on 14 May 1886 in Islington, London, one of the eleven children of James and Mary Ann Emery. It seems that they moved to Alton in about 1900 when James Emery opened The Welcome restaurant at No. 43 High Street, premises currently occupied by Specsavers.

Walter enlisted in the 2nd/4th Hampshires early in the Great War, married Bertha Brown at St Mary's church, Bentworth on 6 May 1915 and a couple of years later they had a son. Ronald Walter was born at Holt End in Bentworth, although by this time his father was serving in Palestine.

The advance on Jerusalem had been held up at Nabi Samweil, the burial place of the Prophet Samuel, which was captured on 21 November 1917. The Turks were keen to retake the village and bitter fighting took place over the next two days. The losses were heavy, with a battalion of Gurkhas, comprising between 800–1,000 men, having only one officer and sixteen men unhurt and the 2nd/4th Hampshires losing two officers and twenty-four men with five officers and eighty men wounded. Jerusalem fell to General Allenby on 9 December and two days later he entered the city on foot, as a gesture of humility and out of respect for the religions to which the Holy City was sacred.

Walter's eldest brother, William, had died in the Boer War; another brother, Robert, died in 1907 whilst serving in India; a third, Leonard, served in the Norfolk Regiment and survived the Great War; whilst a fourth, Frederick, also served in the Norfolk Regiment and was taken prisoner in the Great War and repatriated in 1919. If that was not enough, another brother, Albert, served in the London Regiment and was killed on 31 July 1917, the first day of the Battle of Passchendaele.

Back home things were also bleak for the family as Walter's wife, Bertha, died in Bentworth on 20 November 1918 during the influenza epidemic, leaving their 18-month-old son Ronald to be brought up by her sister.

—— SECOND LIEUTENANT EDWARD JOHN STEWART ——

Second Lieutenant Edward John Stewart, killed in France on November 29, aged 24, was the eldest son of Mr Edward Stewart of Alton, solicitor and agent of the Unionist Party in East Hants. Educated at the Ipswich Middle School, Collyer's, Horsham and Eggar's, Alton he was for some time in the Cambridge and Bradford on Avon branches of the Capital and Counties Bank, and afterwards entered Messrs Coutts and Co. A member of the Civil Service Rifles at the outbreak of war, he proceeded with his regiment to the front in March 1915 and was present at Festubert, Loos and Vimy Ridge. He was sent home with trench fever, obtained a commission in the Machine Gun Corps and joined his company at the front last spring.

HH&AG, 14 December 1917

—— CORPORAL WITHERS KILLED IN PALESTINE ——

It is officially notified that Corporal Harry Withers, second son of Mrs Withers and the late Mr J. Withers, Ethemond, Mount Pleasant Road, Alton, has been killed in action in Palestine.

The deceased soldier had seen much service. He had served in the local Territorials prior to the war, when he was employed at Bognor. He immediately responded to the call and re-joined a few days after war was declared. He proceeded to the Dardanelles in July 1915 and was in several engagements being eventually invalided home with enteric fever in November 1915. On recovery he again went through an arduous training, and was drafted to Palestine in October 1916. He was soon in action and, after seeing a good deal of fighting, was wounded in the head at the Battle of Gaza in March last. He was in hospital in Alexandria and soon recovered. In his letters home he was cheerfully looking forward to 'doing something and having another go at Johnny Turk'.

He was one of Alton's sporting boys and as a lad was identified with the Church Lad's Brigade. He and his brother Ted, now serving with the Australian Forces in France, were stalwarts of the Alton Excelsior Football Club. The deceased was a very popular and promising player and gave many sparkling displays at centre half on the Alton Butts, especially in the season 1911–12 when the local club won the league shield. Another brother, Phil, is also serving in France being in the Wireless Service, RE [Royal Engineers].

HH&AG, 14 December 1917

WOMEN WORKERS ON THE LAND

Alton and the district round about has good reason to be proud of the women who have taken the places of the men who have been called away. In ploughing, the pulling of mangolds and the ordinary work of the farms in this neighbourhood, they continue to do yeoman service and their adaptability and skill in doing the irksome and yet indispensable work of the farm has won our undying gratitude. Who would have thought it possible a few years ago that women

60. Land Army Girl herding cows on a farm in the Alton-Basingstoke area.

61. A female bus conductor looks out of an Aldershot & District Traction Co. Ltd bus that seems to have left a country road.

could have taken the place of men? But they have done it, and done it well, and have faced the rigours of the climate with tenacity and undaunted enthusiasm. We are indeed grateful to them. We have referred to this matter because we hope that it may be possible later on, when a suitable opportunity offers (by a demonstration or the presentation of rewards) to make public recognition of the sterling work which these workers have done in our own district and in other parts of Hampshire.

HH&AG, 14 December 1917

ALTON'S LENGTHENING ROLL

With sincere regret we have to announce the death at the front of another Altonian on 29 November – Pte Charles Harris of the Middlesex Regiment, who lived at No. 4 Plevna Place, Spitalfields Road, Alton. He joined up two years ago.

In February last year he was invalided home suffering from rheumatic fever and loss of speech. By July he had recovered sufficiently to be able to return to France and in his letters home he said he was getting on alright and looking forward to the time he would be able to get leave. Only three days before his death, Mrs Harris received a letter saying he was going into the trenches.

62. Charles Harris and Ethel Stenning were married at the Congregational Chapel in
Normandy Street on 4 July 1914, just a few days after the assassination of Archduke
Ferdinand and his wife in distant Sarajevo.

Deceased, who had just passed his 28th birthday, was formerly in the employ
of Messrs Pilcher & Sons of Market Street. He leaves a widow and one child for
whom much sympathy is felt.

HH&AG, 21 December 1917

IN MEMORIAM

In ever loving memory of my dear husband Pte Charles Harris who was killed
in action on 27 November 1917 aged 28:

> One by one the links are slipping
> One by one old heroes fall
> And you my darling husband
> Have answered the great Roll Call

> From his sorrowing wife and little one.

HH&AG, 28 December 1917

63. Charles Harris, his wife Ethel and baby son, Victor, in 1916. Charles died at Passchendaele in the autumn of 1917.

DROWNED OFF THE HOOK OF HOLLAND

It is with much regret we have to announce the death of Stoker A.C. Page (HMS *Torrent*), who joined the Navy in 1913 and has been on Torpedo Boat Destroyers since the beginning of the war. His boat was sunk off the Hook of Holland on 23 December last. He was 24 years of age, and was the only son of Mr & Mrs Page of No. 24 Laburnum Road, Aldershot, who lived in Alton for many years. He comes from a family of Altonians who have done their bit for King and Country. One cousin went down on the *Good Hope*; another was killed at Mons and a third at Basra.

HH&AG, 4 January 1918

HMS *Torrent* was one of eight Harwich destroyers that formed part of a convoy returning to Britain in December 1917. Three of the ships – *Torrent*, *Surprise* and *Tornado* – were sunk after they struck mines while travelling in bad weather. A fourth ship, *Valkyrie* (the first to strike the enemy mines), survived and was towed home. The destroyer *Radiant* picked up survivors but some 252 officers and men died in the incident. Only three members of HMS *Torrent*'s crew survived and Stoker First Class Alfred Page of Alton died along with sixty-seven comrades.

CHAPTER FIVE

1918

---— KILLED IN MESOPOTAMIA ———

We regret to report that Pte Henry Umpton Poynter, of the Hampshire Regiment, who was reported missing in Mesopotamia, has now been reported killed. He was 27 years of age and the only son of Mr & Mrs H. Poynter of Bow Street, Alton. He served his apprenticeship with Mr Thrower of Alton and at the time of joining up was in the employ of Mr Cheeseman of Cranleigh. He was an 'old Territorial', went to New Zealand, and returned home just before war broke out, volunteered for service and was sent to India, afterwards proceeding to Mesopotamia.

HH&AG, 18 January 1918

64. A 1918 embroidered card souvenir from France.

THE KING'S AFRICAN RIFLES (KAR)

Fighting also took place in German East African (now Tanzania). The King's African Rifles Association website gives a history of the KAR (www.kingsafricanriflesassociation.co.uk/the-history-of-the-kar) and notes that:

> … the enemy did not lay down their arms until November, 1918. By the end of the war the KAR strength had risen to 22 Battalions. This included a 'new' 6 KAR formed from the ex-German askari of the Schutztruppen. The total strength of the KAR was 35,500, of whom 11% were European. Casualties were 8,225, including 22.6% of the officers. The total troops involved were 114,000, with casualties of 62,000. There were between 400,000 and 500,000 native porters – The Carrier Corps, of whom 40,000 were unaccounted for at the end of the campaign.

Stephen Harding, Brother Steven from Alton Abbey, had joined the Norfolk Regiment after being released from his vows and was attached to the KAR. He died from dysentery on 22 January 1918 and was buried in Dar es Salaam, Tanzania.

PRIEST SOLVES MYSTERY OF FLANDERS

'Although sad memories are revived it is a great relief for me to learn that my husband died a brave soldier, and was buried in a decent grave.' This was the comment made by Mrs Allen of Vicarage Road, Alton, Hampshire, on news she had received from Father Joseph Whitaker, a Catholic priest in Liverpool, concerning her husband's fate in Flanders twenty-one years ago.

65. A newspaper report of 1939 revealed that Private J. Allen of the Hampshire Regiment had been buried by the Germans in Steenwerck Communal Cemetery in April 1918. Could the solitary, unnamed CWGC headstone on the far left be his final resting place?

Her husband, Private J.H. Allen, 2nd Hampshire Regiment, was reported missing in France in March 1918. At the time, every effort made by Mrs Allen to find out what had happened to him was of no avail. The only news she received was from the British Red Cross to the effect that he and another soldier had been chosen to deliver an important message during a big attack, and neither had been seen again.

In 1939, Father Whitaker, an artillery officer in the Great War, was able to send her her husband's army pay book and two photographs, still stained with Flanders mud. Father Whitaker wrote:

> When I was in Germany last year, I met a German priest who had been a chaplain during the last war. The German priest told me he had buried your husband in Steenwerck, a village just out of Baillieul, in France. Perhaps, when this war is over, you may be able to visit his grave? The photograph of himself was in another pocket separate from the pay book, and has been pierced by a shell splinter. I wonder if the fine baby, whose photograph he also carried with it, is now grown up.

Mrs Allen replied, 'That baby is grown up and like his father 21 years ago, he is now serving with the forces in France.'

This article appeared in the *HH&AG* on 27 October 1939 and it seems to have been syndicated for it featured in the *News of the World* and as far away as the *Launceston Examiner* in Tasmania.

In Steenwerck Communal Cemetery, not far from the France-Belgium border, there are fourteen graves of named soldiers dating from 1915 and 1916 and five of unnamed soldiers from the Great War. One of the graves of the unnamed soldiers is that of John Allen. His name appears on a memorial to the missing at Ploegsteert a few miles away.

66. The name of Private J. Allen of the Hampshire Regiment, who was killed on 11 April 1918, is included on the Ploegsteert Memorial, which commemorates more than 11,000 British and Commonwealth troops who died in the Great War in this area on the France-Belgium border but have no known grave.

TAKING TO THE SKIES

A few Alton men also served in the Royal Flying Corps and the Royal Naval Air Service, which, on 1 April 1918, were combined to form the Royal Air Force. At the beginning of the Great War, aeroplanes had simply been used for observation. However, they soon started carrying guns to shoot down the enemy's flying lookouts, and bombs to drop on the enemy's troops, ships and factories. Specialised fighting aircraft were then built to shoot down the enemy bombers, and even faster aeroplanes to shoot down enemy fighters.

Every country's newspapers and silent films praised its heroic soldiers and sailors, but pilots were cheered as the dashing, handsome 'stars' of the war. They were called 'aerial duellists' or 'knights of the sky'. These courageous fighters carried no parachutes, and if the aircraft caught fire, they either had to try to crash-land the burning aeroplane safely, or escape the flames by jumping to a quicker death on the ground far below.

67. The Royal Air Force was formed on
    1 April 1918 by merging the Royal Flying
    Corps and the Royal Naval Air Service.

SAPPER LEN POWELL

Sapper L.J. Powell of the Royal Engineers was the first of the Alton men listed on the war memorial of whom I became aware. In the early 1980s, a colleague and I were hosting a Great War project for primary school children at the Curtis Museum and a visitor was very interested in what we were doing, explaining during the subsequent discussion that he had lost his father in the Great War. He returned with a photograph of his parents with him as a toddler, taken during home leave in the spring of 1918. His father, Len Powell, returned to France but was killed shortly afterwards. His mother subsequently received a letter of sympathy from King George V, his medals and a commemorative plaque bearing his name.

The child in the photograph grew up, at one time ran a shop on the corner of Tanhouse Lane and Amery Hill, eventually retired and, in 1984 at the age of 71, Len Powell Junior presented the County Museum Service (as it was then known) with the wartime mementoes associated with his father. These included a metal match-box holder made by his father, recording that he was involved in the Battles at Loos on 25 September 1915, the Somme on 1 July 1916, and Messines on 7 June 1917.

68. Sapper Len Powell of Alton, pictured with his wife and son on his final home leave before returning to the Western Front where he was killed on 2 June 1918.

Although all soldiers dug trenches and holes for their own shelter, the design, construction and maintenance of fieldworks (trenches, strong points, dugouts, duckboards, barbed wire, drainage pipes and pumps) was the job of the Field Companies of the Royal Engineers. Other units also built bridges and roads, and all the huts needed for stores and accommodation. Some detachments operated telephones and other signalling systems, whilst others waged chemical warfare against the enemy. The Battle of Messines was largely won through the efforts of sappers who tunnelled under the enemy trenches and blew them up.

WAR GRAVES IN ALTON CEMETERY

A walk through the cemetery on Old Odiham Road will reveal a number of the distinctive white Portland Stone CWGC headstones, with those closest to Spitalfields Road relating to casualties from the Great War. Whilst some of these are of Alton men whose names appear on the Cairn, the headstone of Rifleman James Spackman of the London Regiment, for example, is different in that he died in the Red Cross Hospital in the Assembly Rooms.

Born in East Molesey, Surrey, early in 1900, James joined the army on 13 April 1915 when he was just 15 years and 3 months old. This was below the official age for signing up but, as he was 6ft tall, James managed to lie convincingly about his age. Following training, he was sent to France and took part in the Battle of the Somme where he was gassed at Gommecourt Wood. He was sent home and, at his father's request, was discharged from army service.

He rejoined the army on 17 May 1917 but later contracted pleuropneumonia at Aldershot and was sent to the Red Cross Hospital in Alton to recuperate. Unfortunately, he had a relapse and died on 26 June 1918. James Spackman was buried in the Old Odiham Road Cemetery three days later, aged 17.

A SCOTTISH VC

Some of our readers will be interested in the announcement that Private Hugh McIver, who was one of the first Royal Scots billeted with Mr S. Pike at No. 77 Ackender Road, Alton, has just been awarded the Victoria Cross.[*]

HH&AG, 16 November 1918

The citation reads:

[*] One of 628 VCs awarded in the Great War.

For most conspicuous bravery and devotion to duty when employed as a company runner. In spite of heavy artillery and machine-gun fire he carried messages regardless of his own safety. Single-handed he pursued an enemy scout into a machine gun post and, having killed six of the garrison, captured twenty prisoners with two machine guns. This gallant action enabled the company to advance unchecked. Later he succeeded at great personal risk in stopping the fire of a British Tank which was directed in error against our own troops at close range. By this very gallant action Private McIver undoubtedly saved many lives.

The London Gazette, 12 November 1918

This conflict took place on 23 August 1918. Private McIver was killed in action near Courcelles in France on 2 September 1918.

LIEUTENANT JOHN ROLLO LOWIS

John 'Jack' Lowis died in Flanders, south of Ypres, on 4 September 1918. The cemetery where he now lies was formed after the Armistice, when graves were transported from isolated sites and smaller cemeteries in the surrounding area. These graves belong to men who were killed between January 1915 and October 1918 and they include many men of the 15th Hampshires and other units who recaptured the area early in September 1918.

Few men named on the Alton War Memorial warranted an inclusion in *The Times* but on 21 September 1918 in their list of fallen officers was included:

Lieutenant John Rollo Lowis, Yeomanry, who was killed in action on 4 September, was the eldest son of the late Hon John Lowis, Government Advocate of Burma, and Mrs J. Lowis, and grandson of the late John Mangles Lowis of Amery House, Alton, Hants. Born in 1893, he was educated at Harrow. Soon after the outbreak of war he enlisted in the Yeomanry, in which regiment he was very shortly given a commission.

John Lowis' next of kin were his parents, the Hon. John Lowis and Monica Lowis of The White House, Fakenham, Kent, so one might wonder why he is listed on the Alton War Memorial.

The Lowis family were an integral part of the Bengal Civil Service for much of the nineteenth century and, by 1891, John Mangles Lowis had retired to Alton where he lived at Amery House (demolished in 1975) with his wife, three married daughters (whose husbands appear to have been serving in Bengal) and some of the grandchildren. A number of family members seem to have died in India, including a daughter in 1900, his eldest son, John, in 1905, and a grandson.

69. Headstone of Captain John Lowis
    at Voormezeele Enclosure, No. 3
    Cemetery, Ypres, Belgium.

70. The Golden Wedding family photograph of John and Ellen Lowis – taken in the grounds
    of Amery House, Alton, on 5 October 1904 – shows the extended Lowis family. Three of
    the boys seen here, grandchildren of John and Ellen Lowis, were killed in the Great War:
    John Lowis (centre row, third from left), Tom Bourdillion (centre row, extreme left) and
    Robin Campbell-Brown (front row, extreme left).

Although John Mangles Lowis died in 1908, aged 80, his widow Ellen remained at Amery House and arranged for a memorial plaque in the adjacent St Lawrence church:

In everlasting memory of
Lieutenant John Rollo Lowis aged 24,
Hants Yeomanry attached 15th Hants Regiment
Temp Major Tom Lowis Bourdillion aged 29
8th King's Royal Rifle Corps
Lt Robin Lowis Campbell-Brown aged 22
8th Trench Mortar Battery
Grandsons of John Mangles and Ellen Lowis of Amery House, Alton
who fell in action in France in the Great War 1917–1918

On her death in 1924, Ellen was buried with her husband in Alton Cemetery.

CORPORAL HERBERT GOODCHILD BOND KILLED IN ACTION

With deep regret we have to record the death in action of Corporal Herbert Goodchild Bond RMLI (son of the late Mr & Mrs Bond, No. 77 High Street, Alton and younger brother of the Revd C.E. Bond), who had lived in Selborne for the past 13 years. Corporal Bond, who leaves a wife and two children, for whom the deepest sympathy is felt, joined up in November last. It is believed that the whole of his platoon went under in the engagement in which he unfortunately met his death. He will be greatly missed in Selborne, where he was intimately connected with the work of the Church. He was one of the lay representatives of the Rural Deanery on the Diocesan Conference, and when residing in Alton was an active worker at All Saints', for many years a server, and from its formation an active member of the Church Lads' Brigade. His widow and brother (Revd C.E. Bond) have received many letters of sympathy for which they are extremely grateful, and regret that, being so numerous, it is impossible to answer them individually.

HH&AG, 1 November 1918

Graincourt-les-Havrincourt, a village 10km south-west of Cambrai, was captured by the 63rd (Royal Naval) Division on 27 September 1918. Corporal Bond died the following day.

DOUGLAS WARNER

Douglas Stewart Warner was born on 10 August 1892 and baptised on 5 June 1893 at the Normandy Street Independent Chapel. He was the son of Louisa and plumber and decorator William Warner.

He married Jessie Agnes Mills, aged 28, at All Saints' church on 26 February 1918 and probably lived in Alton at the time – certainly this is where he enlisted. It is possible that he trained or spent leave in the Colchester area as he married a girl from Rowhedge – which would explain why his name is included on the war memorial there as well as here in Alton.

Douglas Warner died of influenza and pneumonia in the military hospital near Roisel in the Somme region of France on 4 November 1918. Whilst he is buried in Roisel Community Cemetery, he is included on the family headstone in Alton Cemetery.

2ND/4TH HAMPSHIRES

During the 1915–18 Palestine Campaign, the 2nd/4th Hants lost two officers and thirteen men, thirteen officers and 188 men were wounded, and five men were recorded as missing. On Sunday, 26 May 1918, they put to sea for Marseilles and, on arrival there on 1 June, were sent by train north to Bucquoy, between Amiens and Arras in Picardy. They were involved in the Second Battle of the Marne in July and took part in actions near Bapaume in August.

As the advance continued, the Hampshires captured Havringcourt and, in the final stage of the war, the 1st and 2nd/4th Hampshires were part of the main advance eastwards whilst the 2nd and 15th Battalions were engaged in Flanders.

The 2nd/4th Battalion's war diary for 11 November 1918 records:

> At 9 a.m. orders were received that hostilities would cease at 11 a.m. the Armistice having been signed.
>
> It was expected that the possibility of [the] cessation of hostilities would bring a feeling of relief almost overwhelming in its effect. Stranger to say nobody seemed to be excited in the least at the prospect, and it would appear that war with all its horrors and hardships had become the normal state of existence. If outwardly there was little sign of excitement, there could be no doubt that many a man that morning uttered a fervent 'Thank God'.

The 2nd, 2nd/4th and 15th Hampshire Regiments were part of the occupation force in Germany and their regimental history noted that the 2nd/4th had seen more fighting than any other Hampshire Territorial force. The 2nd/4th Battalion was disbanded on 28 October 1919 and their regimental colours were laid up in Winchester Cathedral at a ceremony on Saturday, 12 November 1921.

PEACE BELLS

Not for a long time have the bells of the parish church and All Saints' been heard with such pleasure. 'Sweet charming bells, how many a tale their music tells' and the tale they had to tell on Tuesday was one of the gladness to the heart. We have won a great victory; hearts sore with anxiety can now look around on a world where peace reigns. It was a portent of good news yet received with few extravagant demonstrations in Alton of speech or action. We received it with that modest stillness and humility. And now, when we settle down again, we may turn our thoughts to the conception of a worthy war memorial for Alton and many other subjects which will demand our careful consideration.

Editorial in *HH&AG*, 15 November 1918

Concerning the Great War, an Armistice was signed on 11 Nov. On assembling this morning the Headmaster [Mr Redmond Clark] spoke of its meaning, while the boys sang the National Anthem and Hymns of Thanksgiving. The lessons of the week will be lessons arising from the war and the Peace for which we look in the near future.

Logbook of the National School, now St Lawrence
Primary School, 18 November 1918

THE FLU EPIDEMIC

For some, the war would never end. In over a million British homes at least one man was blinded or crippled or shocked or likely to suffer in some way for the rest of his life. Even after the war was over, thousands of people – both soldiers and civilians – died in the worldwide influenza epidemic.

Of the 318 Canadian troops based in camps on nearby Bramshott and Ludshott commons in the Great War and buried in Bramshott, most died of flu during the winter of 1918/19.

In Alton there were a number of epidemics of influenza during 1918, the first lasting from the beginning of the year until April; the second running from the middle of May through to the end of July. This second outbreak was the most virulent and seven deaths occurred. Dr Bevan, the Medical Officer of Health, reported that, 'almost all houses and the greater proportion of the inhabitants were attacked by it and he could not remember so much sickness at one time with such distress as caused by this epidemic'. Alton does not seem to have suffered greatly in the autumn of 1918 when the vast majority of deaths took place – some 112,329 in England alone.

It is suggested that whilst the Armistice in November 1918 brought an end to the Great War in which 10 million had died, at least 40 million died during the flu pandemic that swept the world at the end of 1918. That it may have had its origins on the Western Front two years earlier has been proposed, which makes the war a contributor.

THE MARCH FROM KUT

Men too weak to walk [were] left to die.

About 135 repatriated prisoners of war from Turkey arrived at Cannon Street Station on Friday last week [20 December 1918]. The majority of them were men who had been taken prisoner at Kut in 1916. In spite of their weak condition at the time of their capture, owing to the hardships of the siege they had just been through, they were at once started on a march which lasted for two months. One soldier said it was quite a common occurrence to see men too ill and weak to march any further, flogged and left to die by the roadside. Every day from 20 to 30 men would fall out and were left with no food and water, to die.

The only food they gave us in the camp was awful; only thin soup and bits of bread. I never saw any solid food for the two years I was a prisoner. Two of my pals went mad through starvation and were then flogged and kicked to death by the guards.

The conditions of the prisoners had, he said, improved greatly during the latter part of 1917. The food continued to be scanty, but this he attributed to lack of organisation rather than any wilful starvation on the part of the Turks, who at the time, really treated them quite well and, in case of sickness, medical attendance was immediately supplied.

Another man said 'We lost over 70% of our men on that terrible march. When men dropped they were chipped on to their feet again, and it was only when they were unable to stand up they were put on camels. There was generally room for fresh men on the back of these animals as so many men were continually thrown off dead as we marched along.'

HH&AG, 27 December 1918

CHAPTER SIX

1919

THE NEXT OF KIN MEMORIAL PLAQUE

Some long-established Alton families have in their possession a 12cm-diameter bronze disc bearing the name of a relative killed in the Great War. Issued in 1919–20 and known colloquially as a 'Death Penny', these memorial plaques were the result of a government scheme to provide a memorial for the next of kin of service personnel who had died on active service.

The plaques were accompanied by a memorial scroll and both items were sent to next of kin separately, accompanied by a letter from King George V which bore a facsimile signature.

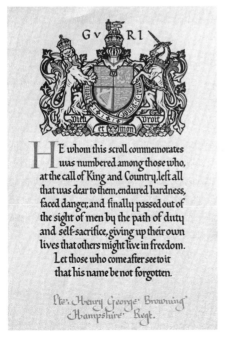

GV RI

He whom this scroll commemorates was numbered among those who, at the call of King and Country, left all that was dear to them, endured hardness, faced danger, and finally passed out of the sight of men by the path of duty and self-sacrifice, giving up their own lives that others might live in freedom. Let those who come after see to it that his name be not forgotten.

Pte. Henry George Browning
Hampshire Regt.

71. A scroll sent from the king to the next of kin of those killed in the Great War, in this case to the parents of Henry George Browning of Alton, who had served in the Hampshire Regiment.

72. Alton Cemetery, showing two gravestones relating to sons lost in the Great War with 'Death Pennies' mounted on them.

In Alton Cemetery there were examples of at least three of these plaques added to gravestones. On the headstone of Alfred and Hannah Norris, the broken-hearted parents of E.L. Norris, who was killed at the Battle of Jutland in 1916, is the only remaining example. Close by, the grieving parents of George and Ernest Small erected a headstone to their two sons bearing the plaque received for George who was killed in France in 1918. Their other son, serving in the Royal Navy died in 1921, a few weeks after the 'qualifying' period. The plaque has been missing from the headstone for many years.

A white marble memorial, in the form of a cross, stood over the grave of F.G. Sumner, who was buried in the cemetery in May 1915, and also bore the plaque sent to his parents. This was photographed in place in March 1985, but it had been removed and the memorial vandalised sometime afterwards.

ALL SAINTS' CHURCH WAR MEMORIAL

Early in 1919 it was suggested that an appeal for two bells and a screen in the church be initiated as a memorial to those men of the parish who had died in the Great War. A report in the local paper indicates that, at a meeting in February, Revd K. McMaster suggested that any memorial should be of benefit to the whole town rather than just the church. Following a discussion, it was agreed that an endowment and naming of a bed in the Inwood Cottage Hospital (formerly in Crown Close at the back of the square – now sheltered housing) would be more appropriate.

In notes on the history of the church provided for visitors, it is mentioned that the calvary outside is a war memorial and that a collection from the congregation (which amounted to £311 10s (£311.50)) was presented to the Inwood Cottage Hospital as a war memorial for two beds to be named 'All Saints' Alton Beds', one in the men's ward and one in the women's.

———————— ALTON POST OFFICE MEMORIAL ————————

To the Alton Post Office belongs the proud distinction of providing the first public memorial in Alton in honour of those members of staff who laid down their lives for their country. The memorial, which occupies a conspicuous position in the General Post Office used by the public, was unveiled on Tuesday evening [29 April 1919] by Mr J.L. Macdonald, Surveyor to the Post Office for the South West District.

The text reads:

> To the Glory of God and in everlasting memory of
> Robert Martin, Sergt Army Service Corps.
> Percy Worsfold, Sergt 1/4th Hants. Regt.
> George Mills, Corpl 10th Hants. Regt.
> Arthur Pickett, L.Corpl 1/4th Hants. Regt.
> Officers of the Alton Post Office Staff
> who in defence of their King and Country
> laid down their lives in the
> World War 1914-1918.
> 'They did their duty even until death.'

Some 24 members of the Alton Post Office staff served in the Army or Navy and they were proud to think that for a small office so many of their colleagues had fought for their country.

HH&AG, Friday, 2 May 1919

The tablet was erected by Mr J.F. Parsons, postmaster of Alton 1890–1919, who had worked for the post office for nearly fifty years. In 1965, when the post office moved from the bottom of Crown Hill to its new building at the other end of the High Street, the tablet was removed. It is now displayed in the Public Collection area of the Royal Mail Sorting Office.

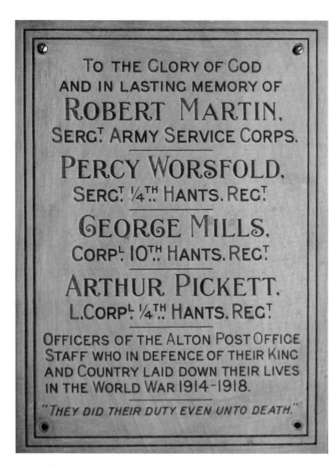

To THE GLORY OF GOD
AND IN LASTING MEMORY OF
ROBERT MARTIN,
SERG.T ARMY SERVICE CORPS.
PERCY WORSFOLD,
SERG.T 1/4.TH HANTS. REG.T
GEORGE MILLS,
CORP.L 10.TH HANTS. REG.T
ARTHUR PICKETT.
L. CORP.L 1/4.TH HANTS. REG.T
OFFICERS OF THE ALTON POST OFFICE
STAFF WHO IN DEFENCE OF THEIR KING
AND COUNTRY LAID DOWN THEIR LIVES
IN THE WORLD WAR 1914-1918.
"THEY DID THEIR DUTY EVEN UNTO DEATH."

73. Alton Post Office Memorial on display in the public collection area of the Alton Royal Mail Sorting Office.

PERCY CHARLES BOND

Percy Charles Bond, the only son of Mr and Mrs C. Bond of Brooke House, Alton, was educated at Eggar's Grammar School and then Cranleigh School. He entered the Capital and Counties Bank (later Lloyds Bank) and in 1915 he joined up as a private in the Public Schools Battalion. He served some time in France and received a commission in the Machine Gun Corps before attaining the rank of lieutenant. In the spring of 1918 he was in the retreat and, at Kemmel Hill, he was gassed and suffered considerably from shell shock. Returned to England, he received treatment in the hospital at Wilton House near Salisbury and spent some time at Osborne House Convalescent Home on the Isle of Wight. Reported unfit for further general service, he returned to light duties and subsequently rejoined his command depot at Alnwick in Northumberland. The troops here were demobilised in February 1919 and Percy returned to Alton. Sadly he died a few months later and his funeral took place on Saturday, 10 May 1919, followed by burial in Alton Cemetery.

──────── PEACE CONFIRMED ────────

The news of the signing of peace reached Alton shortly after 6 p.m. and soon the streets became thronged with people who cheered again and again [at] the gratifying announcement. The Band of the Salvation Army played military airs in the High Street; the Alton Military Band, always alert and ready to help out on patriotic occasions, turned out and, following the cheering crowds, paraded the streets playing popular airs. The Boy Scouts with their Bugle Band were much in evidence; patriotic flags were displayed everywhere, suspended from business premises and private dwellings.

For several hours demonstrative crowds passed up and down the thorough-fares right away to The Butts, from where a procession was formed to the Market Square headed by the Town Band who concluded a capital programme with 'God Save the King' in which the large concourse lustily joined in.

HH&AG, 4 July 1919

──────── THANKSGIVING SERVICE ────────

To be held on The Butts on Sunday, 6 July 1919 at 3.30 p.m. A children's proces-sion headed by the Bugle Band of the Boy Scouts will leave the Market Square at 2.50 p.m. A procession of all the Public Bodies will leave the same place at 3.05 p.m. headed by the Alton Military Band and the Salvation Army Band. A collection will take place in aid of the Alton War Memorial.

HH&AG, 4 July 1919

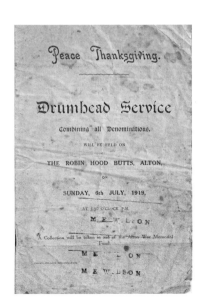

74. Programme for a Peace Thanksgiving Service on The Butts, Alton, 6 July 1919.

———— PEACE CARNIVAL IN ALTON ————

It would be the honest affectation to deny that Alton approached the celebration of Peace Day with somewhat conflicting emotions. There were many things, many evidences of unrest to lessen the Spirit of our rejoicings, many homes in Alton and district where the blow which may have befallen them is so recent, still so keenly felt, that rejoicing at such a time would seem to be a mocking of all we have loved best.

The children who sat down [to a tea] numbered just over 1,000 and several of the relatives of those who fell in the war accepted the invitation of the Committee to join the children. Each child over 4 received a souvenir mug presented by the Committee and supplied by Messrs Hewett and Sons. A few remain in hand, and with the further sum that has since been subscribed it is hoped that it will be possible to present children under 4 with a mug.

The most interest as well as the most striking feature of the day was the Peace Carnival procession which attracted a large number of competitors who showed ingenuity and good taste in the pictorial representations of scenes, periods and characters.

HH&AG, 25 July 1919

At a meeting of the Alton Urban District Council following the Peace Carnival, it was agreed to provide a certificate under their seal on vellum paper to all Altonians who had served in the Great War. This would record the appreciation

75. The Peace Carnival on 19 July 1919 was notable for the rain, but it did not dampen the spirits of those involved.

of the services they had rendered to their King and Country, and the sacrifices they had made. Similar certificates were also presented to the families of those who had died.

CAPTAIN AUGUSTUS AGAR

Although not a casualty of the Great War, Augustus Agar is worthy of mention as he received the Victoria Cross and Distinguished Service Order for his actions with the Royal Navy in the Baltic during the summer of 1919. Agar wrote two books (*Footprints in the Sea* and *Baltic Episode*), which give an interesting account of his service – from 1905 to 1946 – in the Royal Navy. His Victoria Cross is on display in the Imperial War Museum in London whilst the Coastal Motor Boat (CMB 4) in which he won his VC, is on display at the Imperial War Museum, Duxford, near Cambridge. In retirement he farmed strawberries at Hartley Mauditt from 1949, before living in Park House, Alton from 1963 until his death on 30 December 1968. He was buried in Alton Cemetery.

76. Captain Augustus Agar was awarded the VC for an action in Kronstadt harbour on 17 June 1919. Following distinguished naval service in the Second World War, he retired to Hartley Mauditt. Later he moved to Alton where he died on 30 December 1968 and was buried in Alton Cemetery.

—————————— WAR TROPHIES FOR ALTON ——————————

Up and down the country the Government offer of war trophies, pieces of captured military equipment, for safe custody by local communities was not greeted with an excess of enthusiasm; on the contrary, in many instances they were politely but firmly declined.

   As we go to press a meeting is in progress of the Alton Urban District Council, at which an offer is to be considered of war trophies. We have no information as to the precise nature of these gifts, but in accepting (or rejecting) the offer the Council will no doubt be influenced as to whether the gift is a fitting one, in keeping with the dignity of the town and one that should be preserved as a souvenir of the war, which many would like to forget. It must be remembered that Alton rendered important services during the war – it raised large sums of money, men and women worked nobly in providing necessary comforts for the men, for the wounded who were so tenderly cared for in the Alton Red Cross Hospital. In addition, in proportion to its population, Alton raised as many men as any town in Hampshire. We note that the Petersfield Rural District Council, who were offered one German machine gun, one rifle, one bayonet, one water bottle and one mess tin, rejected it as a 'very mean offer'.

HH&AG, 17 October 1919

At the meeting, a letter was read from the War Office, offering the town one field gun, one rifle, one entrenching tool, one water bottle, one helmet and one wire cutter.

WAR SERVICE RECEPTION.

      You are particularly requested to assemble at the Station Approach (Railway Hotel), at 2 p.m. punctually, and fall in in alphabetical order, according to surname, when a procession will be formed and march through the Town headed by The Alton Military Band.

The Certificates will be presented by

General LORD RAWLINSON

(G.C.B., G.C.V.O., K.C.M.G., C. in C. Aldershot Command.)

      If you have not already notified me whether you will be present at the Dinner or not please do so immediately in order that the necessary arrangements may be completed.

26/12/19.   **W. BRADLY TRIMMER,**

Hon. Sec.

77. Invitation to the War Service Reception presentation of certificates on 31 December 1919.

Following discussion, and a suggestion that the gift be refused, the motion to accept the war trophies was carried with one objection. It was suggested that the items should be sent to the Curtis Museum. Despite a proposal that the field gun be positioned in the square behind the Cairn, it was eventually placed outside the Drill Hall on the corner of Albert Road and The Butts. It appears to have remained there until the start of the Second World War, when it was removed for the war salvage campaign. If the smaller gifts did indeed go to the Curtis Museum, there was no trace of them in the early 1980s when new displays were constructed.

ALTON'S SERVICE GUESTS

Presentation of certificates by General Lord Rawlinson*:

The reception given on Wednesday to the men of Alton who were on service during the ever memorable years 1914–1919 by the Alton War Service Committee, as representing the town, was characteristic of the determination of Altonians to render a noble and worthy tribute to those who have so justly earned their recognition. It was no ordinary occasion which called forth their gratitude, and the whole-hearted demonstrations which accompanied Alton's outward and visible expression of thanks and honour – first to the brave dead and secondly, to the survivors who have been spared to return to civil life, left an impression that will long be treasured.

The presentation of beautiful illuminated service certificates followed a march of the men through the town from the railway station headed by the Town Band, and was conducted in the Market Square in the presence of an imposing gathering.

There was a very large muster – some 400 strong – many wearing coveted decorations of service, many partially disabled and one at least who has lost his vision.

HH&AG, 2 January 1920

There followed a substantial dinner in the Assembly Rooms where the guest of honour was Colonel W.G. Nicholson MP and in his speech he mentioned that the honours that came to Alton were '... one CB [Companion of the Order of the Bath]; two Distinguished Service Orders; one Order of the British Empire;

★ General Rawlinson (1864–1925) was given command of the new Fourth Army on 24 January 1916 in preparation for the Allied offensive on the Somme which began on 1 July 1916. He wrote in his diary: 'It is not the lot of many men to command an army of over half a million men.' In November 1919 he was promoted to General Officer Aldershot Command.

four Military Crosses; six Distinguished Conduct Medals; one Distinguished Service Medal; four Military Medals and two Meritorious Service Medals for Gallantry – twenty-one honours in all.'

This was followed by an evening concert.

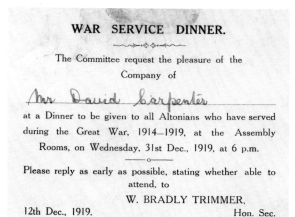

78. Invitation to the War Service Dinner on 31 December 1919.

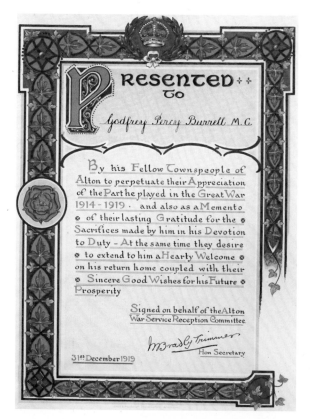

79. Alton War Reception Committee illuminated manuscript presented at the event on 31 December 1919.

Chapter Seven

Post-war

ALTON'S WAR MEMORIAL

At the top of the High Street, on Crown Close, is the Cairn, a unique structure of Cornish granite some 4.5m high, which is generally regarded as Alton's war memorial. However, it is Crown Close and the three buildings around it that are actually the memorial, rather than the Cairn that has been referred to as 'a pile of stones'.

For the full story regarding the choice of Alton's war memorial, please see the article in *Alton Papers 2*, which is also reproduced on the Curtis Museum website.

The Roll of Honour maintained by Revd C.R.S. Elvin bears the names of 187 men who died in what he listed as 'The Great European War'. Interestingly, there are 169 names cast on the bronze panel of the Cairn, although the research for this publication has established the number of dead as 228.

80. Alton Municipal Buildings and War Memorial, *c.* 1920.

Inscribed marble stones were inserted into the High Street wall of both the Assembly Rooms and the Curtis Museum during the last weekend of September 1920 to commemorate their handing over from private to public ownership as part of the war memorial. The former is still in place and acknowledges the generosity of Gerald and Goodwyn Hall. The latter, acknowledging the gift of the Trustees of the Mechanics Institute and the Curtis Museum, was removed in 1985 when building work to improve access to the museum took place. It is currently on display inside the building.

THE MEMORIAL IN ST LAWRENCE CHURCH

From the beginning of the Great War, the vicar had kept a list of all those from the town who were serving in the forces. Almost at once this included the names of those who had died and, from 1915, those names were inscribed on a roll of vellum. When the war ended in 1918, the parish set itself to producing a worthy war memorial, and it was decided that this should take the form of converting the Lady Chapel into the War Memorial Chapel of St Michael and St George.

The proposal was that the south chancel be restored and converted into a Memorial Chapel, that a screen, which should be a copy of the existing fifteenth-century screen, be erected behind the choir stalls (between the chancels) and that a mural tablet be erected for the fallen. Flags were hung in the chapel, including the flag flown all through the war at the Red Cross Hospital, a Union Jack, the White Ensign from HMS *Hermione* and the home-made flag of the local Royal Defence Volunteers. The Altar Cross was given in memory of Alton Red Cross Hospital, 1914–18.

It was finally decided that the roll of vellum already inscribed would make the best form of mural tablet and this was made into the present triptych from the design of Mr H. Kitchin, the architect of the chapel scheme. The chapel was dedicated on 28 November 1920 by Dr Edward Talbot, Bishop of Winchester, although the carved wood and painted figures of St Michael and St George were added in 1927.

SIX HAMPSHIRES KILLED IN IRELAND

Following the delays in enacting the Home Rule Act, 1914, and the Easter Rising by Irish Nationalists in 1916, the Irish War of Independence was considered to be a guerilla war fought by the Irish Republican Army, against the British Government and its forces in Ireland. A number of men in the Hampshire regiments were involved in the fighting and an ambush in Cork saw six of them killed on a mined road:

A detachment of men of the 2nd Battalion Hampshire Regiment, including the band in which Private Washington was a member, were heading to a rifle range near Youghal, Cork for practice when their truck came into contact with a road mine which was electrically detonated [Tuesday, 31 May 1921]. The explosion killed six men and wounded 21 [one died the following day].

As a boy Private Frederick Washington was known for his cheerful and obliging ways; he was a chorister at All Saints' Church [Alton] where he was always present with the choir when he was home on leave. The offer of the Government to convey his remains to Alton for burial was accepted by his family and the body, in charge of a member of the Hampshire Regiment from Ireland, reached Alton on Saturday evening [4 June 1921] where it was removed to the home of his parents in Kingsland Road.

An impressive military funeral took place on Monday, 6 June 1921 and was conducted with solemnity and pageantry of military distinction and it 'sounded a note of triumph amid all that appeared outwardly mysterious and unforgivable'.

HH&AG, 10 June 1921

Another victim of the ambush was 17-year-old Frederick Evans, who lived in Winchester, although his parents formerly lived in Alton where he attended school and was a member of the Church Lads' Brigade. Private Charles Whitear from Alton was also amongst those wounded in the blast.

On 11 July 1921, a ceasefire was announced. By the end of that year, the Anglo-Irish Treaty had been signed ending British rule in most of Ireland.

A DIFFERENCE OF DATES

The Great War is generally regarded as lasting from the government's declaration of war against Germany on Tuesday, 4 August 1914 to the signing of the Armistice on Sunday, 11 November 1918. However, the 'official end' of the war with Germany is taken as the signing of the Treaty of Versailles on Saturday, 28 June 1919, hence the date on the Alton War Memorial as 1914–19.

Nevertheless, British and Commonwealth troops were still engaged in fighting in other areas until the following year. As a consequence, treaties were being discussed with the other belligerent nations, Bulgaria, Austria (both signed in 1919) as well as Hungary and Turkey (both signed in 1920), and these were named after other Paris palaces in which they took place.

The 'qualification dates' for the award of a memorial plaque are 4 August 1914 to 30 April 1920, whilst the relevant dates for the authorisation of Imperial (renamed Commonwealth in 1961) War Graves Commission (CWGC) headstones are from 4 August 1914 to 31 August 1921 under the Termination of the Present War (Definition) Act 1918.

The grave in Alton Cemetery of Private Washington of the Hampshire Regiment, following his death near Cork on 31 May 1921, therefore, has a CWGC headstone. However, the death of Gunner E.J. Small (see below), just four months later on 24 September 1921, does not and he is remembered a few yards away on a family gravestone erected by his parents in memory of him and his brother George, who was killed in action in France in March 1918.

———— DOCKYARD MISHAP AT PORTSMOUTH ————

An accident took place on Wednesday, 21 September 1921, when a party of men were taking ammunition aboard HMS *Renown*, the battlecruiser in which the Prince of Wales was to make his Indian tour. Gunner E.J. Small was crushed between a 15in (381mm) shell (weighing 1,920lbs (872kg)) and the side of the lighter as the shell was being hoisted by a derrick to be swung on board. He died in Haslar Royal Naval Hospital the following Saturday, 24 September 1921.

Only 25 years of age, the deceased artilleryman was born in Alton, where his family lived at No. 20 Mount Pleasant. He received his education at the National School in Normandy Street, Alton, and as a boy was a chorister at All Saints' church, also being a member of the Church Lads' Brigade.

81. Red poppies immortalised by John McCrae's poem 'In Flanders Fields', and adopted by the Royal British Legion as the flower of remembrance.

In 1914 he joined the Royal Marine Artillery and was present on HMS *Valiant* at the Battle of Jutland. At the end of hostilities, E.J. Small saw nine months' service in Ireland. During the last coal strike (in spring 1921) he was engaged on duty in the Scottish coalfields.

He was selected to go with the Prince of Wales on his tour to India as he was described by his commanding officer as '... the best type of a Marine Artilleryman in conduct, bearing and physique'.

The burial of Gunner E.J. Small took place on Thursday, 29 September 1921, following an impressive service at All Saints' church, and he was laid to rest with full military honours in Alton Cemetery. The guard of honour was formed by local Hampshire Territorials and a contingent of Royal Marine Artillerymen. All Saints' church displays a memorial brass plaque to E.J. Small on the wall near the main door.

THE FIRST POPPY DAY IN ALTON

There seem to be no reports of Alton's involvement in the first Poppy Day in November 1921 but the local newspaper does include reference to the formation of a branch of the British Legion:

> A Grand Concert and entertainment is to be given in the Assembly Rooms on Thursday, 24 November 1921 under the auspices of the newly formed branch of the British Legion in which the local branch of the National Federation [of Discharged and Demobilised Sailors and Soldiers] has been merged. The object of the British Legion is briefly to bring together all ex-Servicemen in one fold to make the best use of available resources and to preserve and consolidate that feeling of fellowship which was inspired by the heroic struggles of a never to be forgotten time.
>
> *HH&AG*, 4 November 1921

THE COMMEMORATION OF NAVAL CASUALTIES

At the end of the Great War, the Imperial War Graves Commission considered an appropriate way to commemorate missing naval casualties. They accepted a recommendation that the three naval ports in the UK – Chatham, Plymouth and Portsmouth – should each have an identical memorial – an obelisk which would also serve as a leading mark for shipping. The Portsmouth Naval Memorial on Southsea Common bears the names of 9,666 men who died during the Great War, and was unveiled by HRH the Duke of York (later King George VI) on

82. Portsmouth Naval Memorial on Southsea Common was unveiled in 1924, photographed here in July 2010.

15 October 1924. Lily Weeks, who had lost her husband, William, at the Battle of Jutland, attended the ceremony with her 16-year-old son, Leslie.

——— THE FUNERAL OF MAJOR GODFREY BURRELL, MC ———

Impressive scenes were witnessed at the funeral on Monday of Major Godfrey Burrell MC of Ackender House, Alton who died suddenly aged 50. Major Burrell was an able, honest and sincere man who was educated at Wykeham's School and Winchester College, graduated at Clare College, Cambridge. He joined 4th Battalion Hampshire Regiment in the early 1880s and in 1912 became a Director of Messrs Crowley's, Alton [a brewery formerly located on the site currently occupied by Sainsbury's]. In 1914 he married in Marlborough, New Zealand, Constance Clervaux, fourth daughter of John Clervaux Chaytor, of Marshlands, Marlborough, New Zealand. When the war came it dragged him into its devastating train, as it did many others. He left Alton on 11 October 1914 and was awarded the Military Cross for bravery in leading his men in a drive against the Turks in the Battle of Nasiriyeh, Mesopotamia in July 1915. He was invalided home with dysentery and after seemingly recovering, was again sent out to Mesopotamia. He was again invalided home with the same complaint and he had been more or less an invalid ever since. It was considered a tragic mistake to send him out to Mesopotamia the second time.

His interests were many and his gifts versatile, indeed if it had not been for the handicap of his war experiences he might have made more than a local reputation in some direction – in sport, the natural science or some invention. Constantly he was interesting himself in some new idea or exploring a new avenue of speculation. He possessed the curious mind that sometimes stumbles on greatness.

The funeral procession from Ackender House to St Lawrence Church was watched by hundreds of sympathisers. It was led by a firing party of 11 Platoon (Alton) C Company, 4th Battalion Hampshire Regiment and then came the gun carriage with the coffin which was draped with the Union Jack followed by the pall bearers who were fellow Officers of the Regiment, regimental colour bearers and ex-Servicemen who had served with Major Burrell in Mesopotamia. After the service the remains were laid to rest in Alton Cemetery with full military honours.

HH&AG, 10 July 1931

Godfrey Burrell published a couple of slim volumes which were printed at the Normandy Street printing works of C. Mills, for private circulation amongst his relatives and friends. Entitled *Mixed Pickles* and *Disjointed*, he described them as 'little jottings from my own experience in many places', including some relating to the Great War.

Appendix One

This alphabetical list includes a few facts about each individual; this information is arranged as follows:

Name, date of death, where buried/monument is located, service number, rank, regiment/service, battalion/ship, date of birth (if known), age (if known), Alton War Memorial (AWM), not on Alton War Memorial (X-AWM), All Saints' Roll of Honour (ASRH), St Lawrence Roll of Honour (StLRH), any relevant notes relating to next of kin or employment.

ALBERY, ALBERT

9 June 1918; Bagneux British Cemetery, Gézaincourt, France; 30893; Private; Dorset Regiment; 6th Battalion; AWM.

ALLEN, JOHN HERBERT

11 April 1918; unmarked grave in Steenwerck Community Cemetery, Nord, France, and name appears on Ploegsteert Memorial, Comines, Belgium; 10816; Private; Hampshire Regiment; 3rd Battalion; 28; AWM; son of Mr and Mrs Tom Allen, husband of Mrs May Allen, No. 2 Prospect Place, Alton, joined up 8 September 1914.

ALLWORK, HENRY WILLIAM

17 March 1917; Portsmouth Naval Memorial, Hampshire; J/6264; Leading Signalman, HMS *Paragon*; 23; AWM; son of Henry William and Annie Allwork, No. 2 Plevna Place, Alton, killed in action serving on destroyer in Straits of Dover.

ALLWORK, WYNDHAM JAMES

1 June 1916; Portsmouth Naval Memorial, Hampshire; J/30897; Ordinary Signalman; HMS *Tipperary*; 18; AWM; son of Henry William and Annie Allwork, No. 2 Plevna Place, Alton, killed in Battle of Jutland.

AMOR, WILLIAM

16 May 1919; Alton Cemetery, Hampshire; 26936; Private; Hampshire Regiment; Depot; AWM.

ANDREWS, RICHARD THEODORE M.

Funeral 3 March 1919; Alton Cemetery with Hampshire Regiment; 170413; Sapper; Royal Engineers; AWM; youngest son of Mr and Mrs W. Andrews, Alton, died after a long illness contracted in France.

APPLEFORD, ALFRED CHARLES

24 September 1917; Tyne Cot Memorial, Zonnebeke, Belgium; G/7533; Private; Queen's Regiment, West Surrey; 11th Battalion; AWM; ASRH; grandson of Mrs E. Appleford, Alton, worked for twelve years in Crowley's Brewery.

ARNOLD, HARRY CLEMENT

26 November 1914; Portsmouth Naval Memorial, Hampshire, and included on Holybourne War Memorial; PO/13839; Private; Royal Marines Light Infantry; HMS *Bulwark*; b. Dec 1885; 29; AWM; ASRH; son of William and Emma/Annie Arnold, Holybourne, husband of Annie A.R. Arnold, No. 12 Victoria Road, Alton.

ASLETT, S.

23 August 1917; Tyne Cot Memorial, Zonnebeke, Belgium; 260233; Private; Duke of Cornwall's Light Infantry; 6th Battalion; X-AWM.

ATKINS, EDWIN WALTER

21 March 1918; Arras Memorial, Pas de Calais, France; 32231; Private; Worcestershire Regiment; 14th Battalion (formerly 8193, 2nd Battalion Hampshire Regiment); 28; AWM; No. 14 Tower Street, Alton.

———————— BARNES, WILLIAM ————————

21 April 1917; Faubourg d'Amiens Cemetery, Arras, Pas de Calais,
France; 110853; Gunner; Royal Garrison Artillery; 241st Siege
Battery; 28; AWM; Associate Brother William of Alton Abbey.

———————— BEAGLEY, CHARLES ————————

28 July 1918; Soissons Memorial, Aisne, France; 27715;
Lance Corporal; Hampshire Regiment; 2nd/4th Battalion;
AWM; Normandy Place, Nether Street, Alton.

———————— BEAGLEY, PERCY JAMES ————————

30 January 1917; Vlamertinghe New Military Cemetery, Ypres, Belgium; 33147;
Private; Hampshire Regiment; 14th Battalion (formerly 1649, Hampshire
Yeomanry); b. spring 1887; 30; AWM; fourth of nine children of Herbert
and Kate Beagley, No. 43 Victoria Road, three other sons serving.

———————— BECKINGHAM, REGINALD ————————

25 September 1916; Delhi Memorial (India Gate), India; 3358; Private;
Hampshire Regiment; 2nd/4th Battalion; 19; AWM; son of Mrs Beckingham
of Nether Street, Alton, died following operation for a perforated
intestine, buried at Quetta, Balochistan, India (now Pakistan).

———————— BISHOP, FREDERICK WILLIAM ————————

23 May 1917; Vadencourt British Cemetery, Maissemy, Aisne, France;
115052; Private; Fort Garry Horse; Canadian Mounted Rifles;
23yrs 11mths; AWM; ASRH; son of Edwin Sandel and Sarah Ann
Bishop, No. 9 Vicarage Road, Alton, emigrated to Canada *c.* 1913.

———————— BLUETT, NORMAN RUPERT ————————

1 August 1917; Menin Gate Memorial, Ypres, Belgium; 22510;
Private; Hampshire Regiment; 14th Battalion; 26; AWM;
son of Lionel Rupert and Harriet Bluett, Selborne.

BOLTON, GEOFFREY CHARLES

1 August 1916; Gorre British and Indian Cemetery, Pas de Calais, France; Second Lieutenant, Sherwood Foresters (Notts and Derby Regiment); 17th Battalion; 17; AWM; ASRH; son of Robert Charles and Maud Edith Bolton, Hill House, Alton, trained with the Inns of Court OTC, a server at All Saints' church.

BOND, HERBERT GOODCHILD

28 September 1918; Sucrerie British Cemetery, Graincourt-les-Havrincourt, Pas de Calais, France, and remembered on a family headstone in Alton Cemetery; PO/2533(S); Corporal; Royal Marines; Royal Marines Light Infantry; 38; AWM; ASRH; son of William and Mary Ann Bond, Alton, husband of Ada Mary Bond, Odiham, left a wife and two children, younger brother of Revd C.E. Bond.

BOND, PERCY CHARLES

1 May 1919; Alton Cemetery; Lieutenant; Machine Gun Corps (formerly Public Schools Battalion); 28; X-AWM; only son of Mr and Mrs C. Bond, Brooke House, Alton.

BONE, EDMUND GEORGE

25 September 1915; Ploegsteert Memorial, Comines, Belgium; 8416; Corporal; Royal Berkshire Regiment; 2nd Battalion; 36; AWM; son of Henry and Julia Bone, Alton, served as Brown.

BOWERS, ARCHIBALD ALFRED

1 February 1916; Basra War Cemetery, Iraq; 1963; Lance Sergeant; Hampshire Regiment; 1st/4th Battalion; AWM; ASRH; died of wounds in Persian Gulf.

BOWN, HAROLD J. (YOUNG)

20 June 1915; Basra War Cemetery, Iraq; 2973; Private; Hampshire Regiment; 1st/4th Battalion; 20; AWM; adopted son of Mrs W. Twitchen, Inglewood, Alton, died on board the hospital ship *Madras* of enteric fever contracted in Persian Gulf, previously a clerk in the Union of London & Smiths Bank in Alresford and Winchester, lived in Alresford, on Eggar's Grammar School Roll of Honour.

——— BREWER, WILLIAM GEORGE ———

26 October 1917; Dozinghem Military Cemetery, Poperinge, Belgium; 241717; Private; Gloucestershire Regiment; 14th Battalion; 32; AWM; ASRH; foster son of Beatrice Maria Cox, No. 9 Crescent Villa, Westbrook Road, Alton, died of wounds from action on 24 October 1917.

——— BRIER, VICTOR WILLIAM ———

18 September 1918; Doingt Communal Cemetery Extension, Somme, France, and recorded on Diocesan Bell Ringers' War Memorial, Cathedral Belfry, Winchester; 29171; Private; East Surrey Regiment; 8th Battalion; 19; AWM; adopted son of Henry Brier, Alton, died of wounds in France.

——— BROWN, ROBIN LOUIS CAMPBELL ———
(should be Robin Lowis Campbell-Brown)

29 June 1917; Lijssenthoek Military Cemetery, Poperinge, Belgium; Lieutenant; Royal Field Artillery; 88th Trench Mortar Battery; 21; X-AWM; Amery House, Alton, died of wounds.

——— BROWNING, GEORGE HOWARD ———

13 March 1918; St Leger British Cemetery, Pas de Calais, France; Second Lieutenant; East Lancashire Regiment; 1st Battalion; 22; AWM; son of George and Florence Browning, Marchwood, Southampton, on the staff of the Capital & Counties Bank in Alton, member of Alton Congregational church.

——— BROWNING, HENRY GEORGE ———

26 April 1915; Menin Gate Memorial, Ypres, Belgium; 8491; Private; Hampshire Regiment; 1st Battalion, A Company; b. 1892; 22; AWM; ASRH; son of George Browning and Martha Rapkins (m. 9 Jan 1892), No. 41 Connaught Terrace, Mount Pleasant, Alton, stepbrother of Mr W. Rapkins, Alton, well-known local athlete, awarded Cross Country Medal for regiment in 1912.

BURNEY, GILBERT EDWARD

27 September 1915; Chocques Military Cemetery, Pas de Calais, France; Lieutenant; Gordon Highlanders; 8th Battalion; 24; X-AWM; younger son of Brigadier-General and Mrs Burney, Langham Lodge, Alton, died of wounds in France.

CAPPLEHORN, WILLIAM

28 April 1915; Helles Memorial, Turkey; 9654; Private; Hampshire Regiment; 2nd Battalion; 21; son of Mrs L. Capplehorn, No. 12 Albert Road, Alton.

CARRATT, FREDERICK JOHN

14 January 1917; Philosophe British Cemetery, Mazingarbe, Pas de Calais, France; 1504; Lance Corporal; Royal Fusiliers; 1st Battalion; 26; AWM; ASRH; son of Peter and Jane Carratt, Alton, died on the Somme.

CEMERY, ARTHUR FRANK

19 July 1917; Cojeul British Cemetery, St Martin-sur-Cojeul, Pas de Calais, France; Captain; East Yorkshire Regiment; 1st Battalion; 26; AWM; ASRH; son of captain and Mrs John B. Cemery of Reading, native of Alton.

CEMERY, PERCIVAL CONRAD

21 January 1916; Basra Memorial, Iraq; 701; Sergeant; Hampshire Regiment; 1st/4th Battalion; 26; AWM; ASRH; fourth son of Captain and Mrs J.B. Cemery, killed in action at Orah, Mesopotamia, worked for Messrs Crowley & Company.

CHAWNER, ALAIN PERCY MARK

21 October 1916; Bernafay Wood British Cemetery, Somme, France; Lieutenant; Essex Regiment; 3rd Battalion, attd 1st Battalion; 22; X-AWM; son of Major Hampden and Jeanne Chawner (née Lederrey), Shotters, Alton, educated at Haileybury, enlisted in East Surrey Regiment, August 1914.

CHAWNER, MEREDITH ANDRÉ

21 May 1917; Orange Trench Cemetery, Monchy le Preux, Pas de Calais, France; Captain; Essex Regiment; 21; X-AWM; son of Major Hampden and Jeanne Chawner (née Lederrey), Shotters, Alton.

CHESTERFIELD, BEN F.

21 January 1916; Basra Memorial, Iraq; 3025; Private; Hampshire Regiment; 1st/4th Battalion, H Company; AWM; killed in Persian Gulf, on Eggar's Grammar School Roll of Honour.

CHESTERFIELD, LEONARD S.

11 May 1915; Basra Memorial, Iraq; 3026; Private; Hampshire Regiment; 1st/4th Battalion, H Company; 21; AWM; youngest son of Mr T. Chesterfield, Alton, drowned in Persian Gulf, had been an apprentice dentist in Winchester, on Eggar's Grammar School Roll of Honour.

CHRISTMAS, ARTHUR

31 May 1916; Portsmouth Naval Memorial, Hampshire; K/5656; Petty Officer Stoker; HMS *Queen Mary*; 33; AWM; son of Timothy and Frances Christmas, Alton, killed in the Battle of Jutland.

CLARKE, HAROLD

21 January 1916; Basra Memorial, Iraq; 200696; Private; Hampshire Regiment; 1st/4th Battalion, H Company; AWM; killed at El Hamuc, Mesopotamia.

CLARK, SIDNEY WILLIAM

21 January 1916; Basra Memorial, Iraq; 200694; Private; Hampshire Regiment; 1st/4th Battalion, H Company; AWM; Clevedon, Anstey Road, Alton, died in Mesopotamia.

COLE, EDWARD THOMAS

13 May 1915; Menin Gate Memorial, Ypres, Belgium; 6098; Sergeant; 2nd Dragon Guards (Queen's Bays); X-AWM; son of Thomas and Frances Cole, Hampstead, London, formerly of Alton.

COLE, WILLIAM

17 December 1918; Alexandria (Hadra) War Memorial Cemetery, Egypt; 10509; Lance Corporal; Hampshire Regiment; 1st/8th Battalion; 39; AWM; ASRH; husband of M. Cole, No. 45 Butts Road, Alton, had five children, worked for Messrs Crowley & Company, joined up September 1914, died of pneumonia.

COLEMAN, ARTHUR

24 February 1917; Basra Memorial, Iraq; 200244; Private; Hampshire Regiment; 1st/4th Battalion; 24; AWM; son of William Samuel Coleman, No. 5 Amery Hill, Alton, killed in Mesopotamia.

COLLINS, HARRY

17 April 1918; Camberwell (Forest Hill Road) Cemetery, London; 30102; Private; Royal Inniskilling Fusiliers; 7th/8th Battalion; 34; X-AWM; son of Frank and Annie Collins, Alton, husband of Mrs K. Collins, No. 7 Philip Road, Peckham Rye, London.

COLLINS, LEWIS FRANK

26 January 1918; Fremantle Cemetery, Perth, Australia; 4785; Private; Australian Infantry; 48th Battalion; b. August 1876; 41; X-AWM; joined up in Perth, 11 November 1915, reached Western Front 14 August 1916, wounded 1 September 1916, sent to hospital in England then back to Australia for discharge 15 November 1917, husband of Annie Collins, Milford, Surrey.

COOPER, WILFRED GEORGE

23 April 1917; Windmill British Cemetery, Monchy-le-Preux, Pas de Calais, France; 201344; Private; Hampshire Regiment; 2nd Battalion; 19; AWM; son of Joseph George and Rosabella Cooper, Alton, died of wounds.

COZENS, ARTHUR WILLIAM

19 October 1915; Vermelles British Cemetery, Pas de Calais, France; 17082; Lance Corporal; Grenadier Guards; 2nd Battalion; 21; AWM; son of Zacharia and Lydia Mary Cozens, No. 42, Pinehurst Cottages, Farnborough, Hants, Mr and Mrs Cozens were living at Overbury Cottage (near the Golden Pot) when Arthur completed his will on 30 May 1917.

CRAMPTON, EDGAR WALTER

9 October 1917; Tyne Cot Memorial, Zonnebeke, Belgium; Second Lieutenant; Royal Fusiliers; 5th Battalion, attached to 2nd Battalion; AWM; only son of Mr and Mrs Walter T. Crampton, No. 62 Chandos Avenue, Whetstone, London, formerly of Beech, on Eggar's Grammar School Roll of Honour.

DEADMAN, WILLIAM

16 October; Alton Cemetery; former Private; [?10th] Hussars; 29; X-AWM; invalided home from India, March 1917, died at his parents' house, Beula Cottage, Beech.

DICKER, FREDERICK W.

8 January 1917; Amara War Cemetery, Iraq; 4153; Private, Hampshire Regiment; 1st/4th Battalion; 21; AWM; only son of Mr and Mrs F. Dicker, Alton, died in Mesopotamia.

DOE, CHARLES LEONARD

9 August 1916; Potijze Chateau Wood Cemetery, Ypres, Belgium; 5720; Lance Corporal; Hampshire; 2nd Battalion, C Company; 37; AWM; ASRH; son of James and Anne Doe, Alton, husband of Edith M. Doe (née Dymond), No. 9 Poulson Place, Middlebrooks, Winchester, left a wife and three children, gassed.

DOWNER, F.

AWM.

DYER, EDWARD ARNOLD

28 June 1915; Twelve Tree Copse Cemetery, Turkey, and a family memorial in St Lawrence church (under tower); Lieutenant; King's Shropshire Light Infantry; 9th Battalion, attd 1st Battalion, Border Regiment; 41; AWM; ASRH; eldest son of Edward Dyer, St Helen's Road, Hastings, formerly of Hill House, Alton, died at Gallipoli, on the Eggar's Grammar School Roll of Honour.

ELLIS, ALBERT ANTHONY

29 July 1918; Soissons Memorial, Aisne, France; 241192; Private; Devonshire Regiment; 5th Battalion, D Company; 22; AWM; son of Mr and Mrs Albert Ellis, No. 9 Mile End Road, Highweek, Newton Abbot, Devon, formerly worked at Courage's Brewery.

ELLISON, EDWARD

20 January 1916; Lijssenthoek Military Cemetery, Poperinge, Belgium,
and included on Hunsdon War Memorial near Ware, Hertfordshire;
R/7355; Lance Corporal; King's Royal Rifle Corps; 8th Battalion;
23; AWM; son of James and Elizabeth Ellison, Alton, husband of
Susan Ellison, Penlee, Station Avenue, Walton-on-Thames.

EMERY, WALTER FRANCIS

22 November 1917; Jerusalem War Cemetery, Israel, and included
on Bentworth War Memorial; 202677; Private; Hampshire
Regiment; 2nd/4th Battalion; 31; AWM; son of James
Emery, left widow and one child, killed in Palestine.

ETWELL, ALBERT

29 July 1917; Dud Corner Cemetery, Loos, Pas de Calais, France; 62606; Gunner;
Royal Field Artillery; Reserve Division, Trench Mortar Battery; 36; X-AWM;
husband of Frances Etwell, No. 46 Lower Turk Street, Alton, killed in action with
four comrades by a shell north-west of Loos, remains recovered in July 1919.

EVERITT, FRANK EDWARD

20 July 1916; Albert Communal Cemetery Extension, Somme, France;
Second Lieutenant; Australian Infantry; 1st Battalion; 22; AWM; son
of Mr and Mrs James Everitt, No. 4 Moreton Road, South Croydon,
born in Alton, on the Eggar's Grammar School Roll of Honour, before
enlisting in Australian Imperial Force he received training at Moore
College to be a minister in the Presbyterian Church of Australia.

FLOOD, GEORGE FREDERICK

25 August 1916; Lonsdale Cemetery, Authuille, Somme, France; 6821; Private;
Infantry; Machine Gun Corps; AWM; Associate Brother George of Alton Abbey.

———— FOSBURY, JOHN ————

5 November 1915; Philosophe British Cemetery, Mazingarbe, Pas de Calais, France; 2926; Battery Sergeant Major (WO II); Royal Field Artillery; 113th Battery; 31; AWM; son of James and Sarah Fosbury, husband of Elizabeth Fosbury, Alton, died of wounds at La Bassée from prematurely exploding British shell.

———— FOWLER, EDWARD JOHN ————

12 March 1915; Le Touret Memorial, Pas de Calais, France; T/22459; Driver; Army Service Corps; 1st Division Train; AWM; No. 1 Florence Cottages, Kingsmead, Alton, formerly worked for Mr A.J. Hayden, grocer, Alton.

———— FRENCH, ERNEST FREDERICK ————

9 April 1917; Beaurains Road Cemetery, Beaurains-Pas de Calais, France; Z/2504; Corporal; 8th Rifle Brigade; 23; X-AWM; son of Ernest Edward and Ellen French of Bury St Edmunds, native of Alton.

———— FRENCH, PETER GUY ————

14 July 1916; Thiepval Memorial, Somme, France; 7100; Private; Machine Gun Corps; 62nd Brigade; 18; X-AWM; son of Walter and Annie French, Alton.

———— GATES, ADOLPHUS DANIEL JACK ————

26 March 1918; Dernancourt Communal Cemetery Extension, Somme, France; 4852; Private; 11th (Prince Albert's Own) Hussars; 29; AWM; son of George and Charlotte Gates, Nos 1–2 Orchard Lane, Alton, died of wounds at No. 41 Stationary Hospital, Gailly, France.

———— GATES, FREDERICK ————

23 October 1918; Dueville Communal Cemetery Extension, Italy; T2/SR/02679; Lance Corporal; Army Service Corps; 31; AWM; husband of Edith M. Gates, No. 28 Butts Road, Alton, had served for four years, left two children, died of influenza/pneumonia at 9th Casualty Clearing Station, Italy.

GILES, ERNEST WILLIAM

22 March 1918; Pozieres Memorial, Somme, France; 41355;
Private; Royal Inniskilling Fusiliers (formerly 20700,
Hampshire Regiment); 1st Battalion; AWM; ASRH.

GILES, PERCY

13 September 1915; Dunkirk Town Cemetery, France; 18148;
Private; Royal Marines Light Infantry; HMS *Attentive*; AWM;
ASRH; formerly worked for Messrs Crowley & Company.

GILL, FREDERICK

21 January 1916; Basra Memorial, Iraq; 201197; Lance Corporal;
Hampshire Regiment; 1st/4th Battalion; b. 12 July 1895; 20; AWM; late
of Tanhouse Lane, mother living with married daughter (Mrs Fuller)
at Star Inn, Bentworth, missing presumed dead in Mesopotamia.

GILL, HARRY

28 January 1917; Alton Cemetery, Hampshire; 313300; Private; Royal
Defence Corps; 35; AWM; No. 75 Mount Pleasant Road, Alton.

GILLIAM, EDWARD JOHN

21 January 1916; Basra Memorial, Iraq; 200479; Private;
Hampshire Regiment; 1st/4th Battalion; 41; AWM; ASRH;
son of John and Edna Ellen Gilliam, No. 3 Bow Street, Alton.

GILLIAM, FREDERICK G.

22 November 1917; Jerusalem War Cemetery, Israel; 201252; Private;
Hampshire Regiment; 2nd/4th Battalion; AWM; ASRH; son of John
and Edna Ellen Gilliam, No. 3 Bow Street, Alton, killed in Palestine.

GOUGH, EDWARD PERCY

1 April 1918; St. Sever Cemetery Extension, Rouen, Seine-Maritime, France; 40594; Lance Corporal; Royal Dublin Fusiliers; 10th Battalion; 19; X-AWM; youngest son of Edgar and Ellen Gough, Bishops Waltham, formerly of No. 1 Tower Street, Alton, a native of Wield.

GRAY, LEWIS (LOUIS?) ROCHE

9 May 1915; Ploegsteert Memorial, Belgium; 9133; Private; East Lancashire Regiment; 2nd Battalion; X-AWM; grandson of R. Gray, No. 51 Victoria Road, Alton, son of Frederick William Gray, Wandsworth, killed while dressing comrade's wounds.

GRIERSON, JAMES

19 August 1918?; Ploegsteert Memorial, Belgium; 9499; Private; Border Regiment; 1st Battalion?; AWM; Associate Brother James of Alton Abbey.

GUNNING, JAMES W.

1 April 1916; Boatswain's Mate; HMAT *Euripides*; 31; AWM; ASRH; son of Mr and Mrs A.H. Gunning, Ackender Road, Alton, died of fever contracted in the Persian Gulf.

HAGGER, BERNARD WILLIAM

27 November 1917; Kantara War Memorial Cemetery, Egypt; 201706; Corporal; Hampshire Regiment; 2nd/4th Battalion, C Company; 21; AWM; son of William and Mary A. Hagger, 'Sans Souci', Ernest Road, Hornchurch, Essex, native of Stratford, London, enlisted in Alton.

HARDING, CLAUDE STEPHEN

22 January 1918; Dar Es Salaam War Cemetery, Tanzania; Lieutenant; Norfolk Regiment, attd King's African Rifles; 4th/4th Battalion; 30; AWM; Brother Stephen of Alton Abbey, son of Annie Harding, No. 42 Hardy Road, Blackheath, London, and Cecil Murray Harding.

HARDING, JACK

16 November 1914; Deal Cemetery, Kent; K/4666; Petty Officer Stoker First Class; HMS *Viking*; 23; X-AWM; son of Mr and Mrs A.E. Harding, New Cottages, Old Odiham Road, Alton, lived at East Worldham and appears on the village war memorial.

HARRIS, CHARLES THOMAS

29 November 1917; Tyne Cot Memorial, Zonnebeke, Belgium, and on war memorial at Fairford, Gloucestershire; TF/42301; Private; Middlesex Regiment; 1st Battalion; 29; AWM; No. 4 Plevna Place, Spitalfields, Alton, left a wife and one son, employee of Messrs Pilcher and Sons, Market Street.

HARRISON, FREDERICK CHARLES

24 July 1915; Basra War Cemetery, Iraq; 2675; Private; Hampshire Regiment; 1st/4th Battalion; AWM; a clerk at Treloars Cripples College, Alton, killed in Persian Gulf.

HASLETT, WILLIAM GEORGE

Hampshire Regiment; ?2nd/4th Battalion, H Company; AWM.

HAWKINS, STEPHEN

12 February 1918; Duisans British Cemetery, Etrun, Pas de Calais, France; T/16463; Farrier Staff Sergeant; Army Service Corps; 35; AWM; son of Mr J. Hawkins, No. 71 Ackender Road, Alton, husband of Anna Mary Hawkins (née Earle), No. 9, St Mels Road, Longford, died of septic poisoning at 19th Casualty Clearing Station.

HAY, WILLIAM

11 April 1916; Avesnes-Le-Comte Communal Cemetery, Pas de Calais, France; 577; Sergeant; Corps of Military Police; 4th Division, Mounted Branch; AWM; son of John and Mary Hay, Bow, London, wife formerly lived in Langham Cottage, Kingsland Road, Alton, died of wounds.

——— HEATH, FRANK ERNEST ———

14 May 1919; Croydon (Queen's Road) Cemetery, Surrey; 5710; Private;
The Buffs (East Kent Regiment); 2nd Battalion, A Company; 39; X-AWM;
son of John and Elizabeth Heath of Alton, husband of E.A. Heath,
No. 14 Beverley Road, Anerley, London (born in Beckenham, Kent).

——— HEATH, HENRY JAMES, MC ———

1 July 1916; Hawthorn Ridge Cemetery No. 1, Auchonvillers,
Somme, France; Lieutenant; Middlesex Regiment; 16th Battalion; 39;
X-AWM; son of George and Eliza Barbara Heath, born in Alton.

——— HETHERINGTON, GEOFFREY NEVILL ———

21 April 1918; Boulogne Eastern Cemetery, Pas de Calais, France; 81279;
Private; Durham Light Infantry; 15th Battalion, B Company; b. 1889;
18; AWM; son of Walter H. and Margaret Hetherington, Chilland, near
Winchester, Hants, born in Alton, called up on 29 September 1917.

——— HETHERINGTON, GUY ———

27 March 1917; Jerusalem Memorial, Israel; Captain; Essex Regiment;
7th Battalion; b. 1894; AWM; ARRH; son of Mrs A.C. Hetherington,
Eastbrook House, Alton, Eggar's Grammar School Roll of Honour.

——— HICKMAN, G. ———

6 February 1918; Chocques Military Cemetery, Pas de Calais, France;
128178; Gunner; Royal Field Artillery; X42nd Trench Mortar Battery;
26; X-AWM; son of G. Hickman, No. 15 Turk Street, Alton.

——— HOLE, HUBERT FENTON ———

30 June 1916; Basra Memorial, Iraq; 200606; Private; Hampshire
Regiment; 1st/4th Battalion; AWM; died as Turkish prisoner of war.

HOPWOOD, MARCUS

3 September 1915; Thiepval Memorial, Somme, France; Second Lieutenant; Royal Sussex Regiment; 13th Battalion; 28; AWM; No. 2, The Beeches, The Butts (since renumbered as No. 84 The Butts) Alton, bank clerk in Alton, killed in action during an attack on Becourt Ridge.

HORLOCK, ERNEST GEORGE, VC

30 December 1917; British Military Cemetery, Hadra, Alexandria, Egypt, and memorial in St John's church, Langrish, Petersfield; 42617; Battery Sergeant Major; Royal Field Artillery; b. 24 October 1885; 32; X-AWM; son of John and Emily Horlock, No. 5 Fitzlan Road, Littlehampton, enlisted 22 February 1914, drowned following loss of MHT *Aragon*. Memorial by the Cairn, Alton, unveiled 15 September 2014.

HORLOCK, JOHN HARRY

24 January 1916; Kut War Cemetery, Iraq; 8214; Private; Dorsetshire Regiment; 2nd Battalion; 29; X-AWM; son of John and Emily Horlock of No. 5 Fitzlan Road, Littlehampton, born at Beech Farm, Alton, died of pneumonia.

HOSKINS, FRANCIS DESMOND

30 September/1 October 1915; Poperinge New Military Cemetery, Belgium; Second Lieutenant; North Staffordshire Regiment; 1st Battalion; 19; X-AWM; younger son of Mrs H. Hoskins, No. 60 Ackender Road, Alton, killed in Flanders.

HURLOCK, HENRY, DSM

22 November 1916; Portsmouth Naval Memorial, Hampshire; 238126; Leading Seaman; HM Submarine *E30*; b. 8 April 1890; 26; AWM; son of James Hurlock, Headley, husband of Rose Elizabeth Hurlock, No. 33 Testwood Road, Southampton, born in Alton.

HURLOCK, WILLIAM J.

13 August 1915; Helles Memorial, Turkey; 6422; Lance Corporal; Hampshire Regiment; 2nd Battalion; AWM; died in sinking of HMT *Royal Edward*.

JACKSON, JOSEPH

13 October 1915; Loos Memorial, Pas de Calais, France; 6821; Private; Northamptonshire Regiment; 1st Battalion; 32; AWM; son of Enoch and Lucy Jackson, Coventry, husband of Jessie Alice Jackson, Turk Street, Alton, formerly worked for Courage's Brewery.

JEFFERY, TOM FORBES

16 April 1918; Mendinghem Military Cemetery, Poperinge, Belgium; Second Lieutenant; Royal Field Artillery; 19; AWM; son of Mr and Mrs George Jeffery, Bank House, Alton, died of wounds.

KEELING, GEORGE THOMAS

31 May 1916; Portsmouth Naval Memorial, Hampshire; 236625; Leading Seaman; HMS *Black Prince;* AWM; No. 10 Woodbine Cottages, Anstey, Alton, killed in the Battle of Jutland.

KENWARD, WILLIAM THOMAS

22 August 1917; Tyne Cot Cemetery, Zonnebeke, Belgium, and on war memorial at Fairford, Gloucestershire; 285208; Private; Oxfordshire and Buckinghamshire Light Infantry; 2nd/1st Battalion; 35; AWM; husband of Annie Kenward, No. 14, Vicarage Road, Alton.

KEYWORTH, CLEMENT ROBINSON

5 August 1916; Thiepval Memorial, Somme, France; 2521; Private; The King's (Liverpool Regiment); 1st/9th Battalion; 29; X-AWM; son of Frederick William and Ellen Keyworth, Sheffield, husband of Marjorie Keyworth, No. 5 Market Square, Alton.

KNIGHT, ERNEST WILLIAM

3 March 1915; Menin Gate Memorial, Ypres, Belgium; Y/477; Rifleman; King's Royal Rifle Corps; 3rd Battalion; 25; AWM; son of Mr and Mrs G. Knight, Alton, No. 8 Victoria Road, Alton, well-known footballer who played for Alton Excelsiors.

KNIGHT, F.G.C. (FRANCIS GEORGE)

31 May 1916; Portsmouth Memorial, Hampshire; Acting
Leading Stoker; HMS *Queen Mary*; X-AWM; parents lived in
Normandy Street, Alton, killed in the Battle of Jutland.

KNIGHT, FREDERICK CHARLES

4 October 1917; Poelcapelle British Cemetery, Belgium; 25322;
Private; Hampshire Regiment; 1st Battalion; 30; X-AWM; son of
James and Emma Knight, Alton, husband of Flora Elsie Knight
(née Heilbron) of Basingstoke, No. 1 Vicarage Road, Alton.

KNIGHT, GEORGE JAMES

4 October 1916; Thiepval Memorial, Somme, France; 23791; Private;
Wiltshire Regiment; 1st Battalion; X-AWM; No. 52 Woodland
Terrace, Victoria Road, Alton, came from Cliddesden in 1914.

LASSAM, EDWARD JOHN

1 July 1916; Thiepval Memorial, Somme, France; 9426; Private; Hampshire
Regiment; 1st Battalion; 24; AWM; son of Mr and Mrs George Lassam,
Eastern Cottage, Paper Mill Lane, Alton, joined up October 1913.

LAWRENCE, REGINALD ARTHUR

31 August 1918; Sucrerie Cemetery, Ablain St Nazaire, Pas de Calais, France;
45520; Rifleman; Rifle Brigade; 12th Battalion; 22; AWM; son of Frederick and
Susan Lawrence, No. 7 Cambridge Road, Anerley, London, clerk of Treloar
Cripple Hospital, member of Wesleyan church, killed in a bombing raid.

LILLYWHITE, JAMES

1 September 1917; Kirklee 1914–1918 Memorial, Poona, India; 355924; Sergeant;
Hampshire Regiment; 1st/9th Battalion; 40; AWM; husband of Mrs Elizabeth
Lillywhite, No. 4 Lime Kiln Cottages, Wilsom Road, Alton, worked for
Messrs Crowley & Company, died at the station hospital, Ferozepore, India.

LOTT, JOHN ENGLISH

21 May 1917; La Chapelette British and Indian Cemetery, Peronne, Somme, France; Second Lieutenant; Royal Engineers; 4th Field Survey Company, S Section; 42; AWM; son of John and Marion Lott, Woodgates, East Bergholt, Suffolk, Brother John of Alton Abbey.

LOWIS, JOHN ROLLO

4 September 1918; Voormezeele Enclosure No. 3, Ypres, Belgium; Captain; Hampshire Yeomanry (Carabineers); 24; AWM; grandson of John and Ellen Lowis, Amery House, Alton, son of the Hon. John Lowis and Monica Lowis, The White House, Fawkham, Kent.

MAJER, SAMUEL CHARLES

17 October 1918; Highland Cemetery, La Cateau, France; 236411; Sapper; Royal Engineers; 4th Siege Company, Royal Monmouthshire; 31; X-AWM; son of Mrs Bessie Majer, No. 13 Albert Road, Alton.

MARLOW, PERCY

7 June 1917; Klein-Vierstraat British Cemetery, Kemmel, Belgium; Captain; Wiltshire Regiment (The Duke of Edinburgh's); 6th (Service) Battalion; 25; AWM; ASRH; eldest son of Mr and Mrs Henry Marlow, Netherton House, Alton, killed in the Wychaete Battle.

MARLOW, WILLIAM 'WILL' GEORGE

26 May 1917; Abbeville Communal Cemetery Extension, Somme, France; Y/478; Sergeant; King's Royal Rifle Corps; 7th Battalion; 29; AWM; ASRH; only son of Corporal and Mrs M. Osgood, No. 23 Butts Road, Alton, died in No. 1 South African General Hospital, Abbeville, France.

MARTIN, ERNEST

8 January 1918; Poelcapelle British Cemetery, Belgium; 123201; Private; Machine Gun Corps; 214th Company; 19; X-AWM; son of John and Eva Martin, Anstey Manor, Alton, born in Milton Abbas near Blandford Forum, Dorset.

—— MARTIN, ROBERT AMBROSE JESSIE ——

10 December 1918; Ste Marie Cemetery, Le Havre, Seine-Maritime, France, and remembered on the post office memorial plaque, Royal Mail Sorting Office, Alton; S/20568; Sergeant; Royal Army Service Corps; Base Supply Depot (Le Havre); 33; AWM; son of Frederick and Rhoda Maria Martin, Alton, husband of Nellie Martin, Chichester, father of two, lived at No. 7 Youngs Road, Alton, died of pneumonia after contracting flu, served all his time in France after being called up at start of the war, formerly a postman at Privett and Binsted.

—— MASON, ALBERT EDWARD ——

24 October 1914; Le Touret Memorial, Pas de Calais, France; 7974; Lance Corporal; South Lancashire Regiment; 2nd Battalion; b. 28 October 1886; 29; AWM; Orchard Terrace, Alton, son of T.E. and Ada Mason, Smart's Hill, Penshurst, Kent, reported missing 24 October 1914, death confirmed March 1916, worked for Messrs Crowley & Company.

—— MCARTHUR, ROBERT ——

1 October 1918; Ledeghem Military Cemetery, Belgium; S/1913; Corporal; Seaforth Highlanders; 7th Battalion, C Company, Trench Mortar Battery; 34; AWM; son of Mr and Mrs Robert McArthur, No. 126 Stirling Road, Townhead, Glasgow, husband of Jane McArthur (d. 1959), No. 47 Butts Road, Alton, formerly billeted in Alton, m. 1915.

—— MCNEILL, NEIL ——

11 November 1914; Menin Gate Memorial, Ypres, Belgium; Second Lieutenant; Black Watch; 1st Battalion, A Company; 20; AWM; b. 1894 in Yokohama, Japan, educated at Charterhouse and Hertford College, Oxford, gazetted 8 July 1914, went to Belgium on 24 September 1914, killed in action at Polygon Wood, son of Duncan and Emilia Margaret McNeill, Shanghai, medals sold at Christies (lot 264) on 10 November 1992, in 1915 Mrs McNeill living at Snode Hill House, Beech, Alton.

—— MERRETT, ARTHUR EDWIN ——

18 December 1916; Dickebusch New Military Cemetery, Ypres, Belgium; Second Lieutenant; Hampshire Regiment; 15th Battalion; 26; AWM; No. 48 Ackender Road, Alton, son of Ernest and Emma Merrett, Belle Vue, Selborne.

———— MILLER, ALTON JOHN BLACHFORD ————

23 April 1917; Tilloy British Cemetery, Tilloy-les-Mofflaines,
Pas de Calais, France; X/58; Gunner; South African Heavy Artillery;
125th Siege Battery; X-AWM; son of Robert Cato Hall and Kate Inez
Miller, Rand Club, Johannesburg, South Africa, native of Alton.

———— MILLS, BERTIE JAMES HAROLD ————

23 April 1917; Monchy British Cemetery, Monchy-le-Preux, Pas de Calais,
France; 27655; Private; Hampshire Regiment; 2nd Battalion; X-AWM;
son of Edith and the late James Mills, No. 115 Grosvenor Road, Aldershot,
one of three brothers lost in the Great War recorded on their father's
headstone (d. 12 October 1914) in Aldershot Cemetery, born in Alton.

———— MILLS, GEORGE ————

28 April 1917; Salonika (Lembet Road) Military Cemetery, Greece,
and remembered on the post office memorial plaque, Royal Mail
Sorting Office, Alton; 14651; Corporal; Hampshire Regiment;
12th Battalion; 32; AWM; son of Mr and Mrs G. Mills, husband of Ellen
Kathleen Mills, No. 9 Tanhouse Lane, Alton, died of wounds.

———— MITCHELL, NORMAN WILLIAM ————

26 April 1918; Tyne Cot Memorial, Zonnebeke, Belgium; 13082;
Rifleman; King's Royal Rifle Corps; 17th Battalion; 19; AWM;
son of Albert George and Alice Mitchell, No. 3 Westbrooke Road, Alton.

———— MONGER, SYDNEY ————

28 March 1915; Civilian; SS *Fulaba*; 42; AWM; No. 9 Youngs Road,
Alton, employed by Southern Nigerian Government Telegraphs,
ship torpedoed en route from Liverpool to Sierra Leone.

———— MORGAN, HENRY ————

26 November 1914; Portsmouth Naval Memorial, Hampshire; M/6168;
Ship's Corporal First Class; HMS *Bulwark*; 31; AWM; son of Henry and Alice
Morgan, Well House, Beech, killed when ship blew up off Sheerness.

MORGAN, JAMES

18 December 1916; Baghdad (North Gate) War Cemetery, Iraq; 200918;
Private; Hampshire Regiment; 1st/4th Battalion; 21; AWM; son of G. Morgan,
No. 33 Turk Street, Alton, joined up in August 1914, aged 19, wounded
14 December 1915, taken POW at Kut, 29 April 1916, died of disease, previously
employed at Borovere Laundry and sergeant of the Church Lads' Brigade.

MURRANT, WILLIAM CHARLES

11 December 1916; Guards' Cemetery, Combles, Somme, France;
10489; Guardsman, Coldstream Guards; 2nd Battalion; 21; AWM; son
of Mr and Mrs Charles T. Murrant, No. 37 Butts Road, Alton.

NASH, HENRY THOMAS

18 October 1916; Thiepval Memorial, Somme, France; 15246; Private; Hampshire
Regiment; 2nd Battalion; 30; AWM; eldest son of Mrs C. Nash, Locks Cottages,
No. 39 Normandy Street, Alton, formerly worked at Courage's Brewery.

NELSON, ROBERT

24 March 1918; Pozieres Memorial, Somme, France; 14208;
Private; Household Cavalry; 6th Dragon Guards (Carabineers);
AWM; previously a porter at the workhouse.

NEWMAN, CHARLES W.

3 June 1915; Caberet-Rouge British Cemetery, Souchez, Pas de Calais, France;
4796; Private; Connaught Rangers; 1st Battalion; 22; AWM; son of Mr and
Mrs T. Newman, No. 41 Victoria Road, Alton, born at Holloway, London.

NEWPORT, GEORGE WILLIAM

27 September 1916; Thiepval Memorial, Somme, France; 65825; Corporal;
Royal Engineers; 126th Field Company; AWM; ASRH; parents lived
in Queen's Road, Alton, killed by a shell in the Somme advance, left a
wife and seven children, had been member of Alton Fire Brigade.

NORRIS, ARTHUR JOHN

13 November 1916; Thiepval Memorial, Somme, France; PO/16367; Lance Corporal; Royal Marine Light Infantry; 2nd Royal Marine Battalion, RN Division; X-AWM.

NORRIS, ERNEST LEONARD

31 May 1916; Portsmouth Naval Memorial, Hampshire; J/6172; Able Seaman; HMS *Black Prince*; 22; AWM; ASRH; son of Mr and Mrs (Hannah) Norris, No. 24 Ackender Road, Alton, brothers also served, killed in the Battle of Jutland.

NORRIS, GEORGE

25 August 1917; Tyne Cot Memorial, Zonnebeke, Belgium; 5248; Private; Hampshire Regiment; 2nd Battalion; X-AWM.

NORRIS, JAMES

2 October 1915; Plymouth (Efford) Cemetery, Devon; 7670; Private; Hampshire Regiment; 2nd Battalion; X-AWM; died at 4th Southern General Hospital, Plymouth, from wounds received in the East.

OSBOURNE, WILFRED

22 November 1917; Jerusalem War Cemetery, Israel; 201677; Lance Corporal; Hampshire Regiment; 2nd/4th Battalion; 25; AWM; killed in Palestine, previously worked at Mr Caesar's hairdressing shop, High Street, Alton.

OVER, ERNEST

29 August 1918; Vis-en-Artois Memorial, Pas de Calais, France; 315113; Lance Corporal; London Regiment and 2nd Rifle Brigade; 5th Battalion (London Rifle Brigade) attd 2nd Battalion Rifle Brigade; 40; X-AWM; eldest of six brothers who served, son of D.A. Over, Updown Hill, Windlesham, Surrey, husband of Winnie K. Over, Alton.

PACEY, THOMAS

9 August 1915; Portsmouth Naval Memorial, Hampshire; 308295; Stoker First
Class; HMS *Lynx*; 29; X-AWM; son of Edward and Harriet Pacey, No. 15
Vicarage Road, Alton, killed in mine explosion off Moray Firth, Scotland.

PAGE, ALFRED CHARLES

23 December 1917; Portsmouth Naval Memorial, Hampshire; SS/114716;
Stoker First Class; HMS *Torrent*; 24; X-AWM; son of Alfred and Emily
Page, Aldershot, formerly of Alton, native of Alton, joined the navy in
1913, killed by mine explosion in North Sea, off the Hook of Holland.

PAGE, CECIL FREDERICK

31 March 1918; Ramleh War Cemetery, Israel; 201559; Private;
Hampshire Regiment; 2nd/4th Battalion, C Company; 23; AWM;
son of William and Annie Page, husband of Gertrude Kate Page
(née Murray), No. 13 Mount Pleasant Road, Alton, killed in Palestine.

PALMER, ARTHUR W.

14 March 1916; Loos Memorial, Pas de Calais, France; G/740; Private;
The Queen's (Royal West Surrey Regiment); 6th Battalion; 30; AWM;
son of Richard and Mary Ann Palmer, No. 16 Tower Street, Alton.

PALMER, CECIL HOWARD

26 July 1915; Helles Memorial, Turkey; Lieutenant Colonel; Royal
Warwickshire Regiment (formerly of Worcestershire Regiment); CO
9th Battalion; 42; AWM; son of Revd J. and Mrs Palmer, East Worldham
Rectory, husband of Hilda Beatrice Palmer, No. 35 Anstey Road, Alton.

PALMER, DANIEL THOMAS

14 October 1915; Loos Memorial, Pas de Calais, France; 8797;
Private; East Surrey Regiment; 7th Battalion; 43; X-AWM; son of
Frederick Palmer of Alton, Hants, husband of Eliza Gertrude Palmer,
No. 23, Denison Road, Collier's Wood, Merton, London.

——— PALMER, H. (?H.E.) ———

24 July 1915; Basra War Cemetery, Iraq; 3261; Private;
Hampshire Regiment; 1st/4th Battalion; AWM.

——— PARRACK, RICHARD RALPH ———

17 October 1916; Thiepval Memorial, Somme, France; 5698; Private;
Hampshire Regiment; 2nd Battalion; 35; AWM; son of James and Helen
Parrack, husband of Emily Parrack (née Offer), No. 14 Tower Street, Alton, left
three children, previous army service (1902–04), killed in action in France.

——— PAYNE, HENRY ———

28 February 1917; Sailly-Saillisel British Cemetery, Somme, France; 4917;
Sergeant; Royal Fusiliers; 1st Battalion; AWM; son of William and Elizabeth
Payne, Roxeth, Harrow, Middlesex, husband of Sarah Ellen Payne, No. 94
The Butts, Alton, left two children, formerly worked at Courage's Brewery.

——— PAYNE, W.F. (?WALTER) ———

11 March 1918; Erquinghem-Lys Churchyard Extension, France;
9996; Private; South Wales Borderers; 10th Battalion; AWM;
nephew of A. Wateridge, Dukes Head Hotel, Alton.

——— PICKETT, ARTHUR ———

20 July 1918; Marfaux British Cemetery, Marne, France, and remembered
on the post office memorial plaque, Royal Mail Sorting Office,
Alton, headstone in Alton Cemetery erected by his wife; 201678;
Lance Corporal; Hampshire Regiment; 2nd/4th Battalion; 38; AWM;
son of William (verger, All Saints' church) and Elizabeth Pickett,
husband of Bessie Pickett, No. 12 Upper Grove Road, Alton.

——— PILCHER, ERNEST JAMES ———

2 August 1917; Gaza War Cemetery, Israel; 241999; Private; Hampshire Regiment;
2nd/5th Battalion; AWM; previously a sidesman in All Saint's church.

PINK, ARTHUR MORRIS

20 August 1915; Portianos Military Cemetery, Lemnos, Greece; 14289; Private; Hampshire Regiment; 10th Battalion; AWM; No. 14 Amery Street, Alton.

PINK, EDWARD CROFT

25 October 1916; Grove Town Cemetery, Meaulte, Somme, France; 4660; Private; Hampshire Regiment; 1st Battalion; AWM; parents lived at No. 14 Amery Street, Alton, had previously served in India, an old soldier who rejoined on 1 September 1914.

PINK, HARRY

20 May 1915; Alexandria (Chatby) Military and War Memorial Cemetery, Egypt; 9044; Private; Hampshire Regiment; 2nd Battalion; AWM; parents lived at No. 14 Amery Street, Alton.

PIPER, ALFRED STANDEN

1 September 1916; Basra Memorial, Iraq, and mentioned on parents' gravestone in Alton Cemetery; 461206; Private; Royal Medical Army Corps; 1st/4th Battalion, attd Hampshire Regiment, H Company; 23; AWM; son of Alfred and Harriet Piper, No. 48 High Street, Alton, taken prisoner after fall of Kut, 1916, died in Bagdad Hospital, on Eggar's Grammar School Roll of Honour.

PIPER, WILLIAM HENRY SAGE

10 September 1918; Barenthal Military Cemetery, Italy; 323063; Gunner; Royal Garrison Artillery; 197th Siege Battery; 25; X-AWM; son of Alfred Henry and Emily Louisa Piper, Springles Farm, Colaton, Raleigh, Devon, husband of Annette Amy Piper, Old Park Farm, Beech, married at St Lawrence church 24 April 1916, killed by shell in Italy, left one child.

POND, E. GEORGE

17 December 1915; Delhi Memorial (India Gate), India, buried at Quetta Government Cemetery; 2000; Private; Hampshire Regiment; 2nd/4th Battalion; AWM; Church Street, Alton, died at Quetta, husband of Gertrude Pond (née Keal), Allerford, Taunton, Somerset.

POPE, ROBERT JAMES

12 July 1915; Twelve Tree Copse Cemetery, Turkey; 9574; Private; Hampshire Regiment; 2nd Battalion; AWM; killed in Dardanelles, next of kin recorded as H.G. Pope (brother), Royal Marines Light Infantry, Deal, Kent.

PORCH, WILLIAM

1 August 1917; Karasouli Military Cemetery, Greece; 9640; Private; Hampshire Regiment; 12th Battalion; X-AWM; mother lived at No. 35, Church Street, Alton, former employee of Crowley's Brewery, killed at Salonica.

POWELL, LEONARD JOHN

2 June 1918; Bouilly Cross Roads Military Cemetery, Marne, France; 49087; Sapper; Royal Engineers; 94th Field Company; AWM; died of wounds.

POYNTER, HENRY UMPTON

21 January 1916; Basra Memorial, Iraq; 201066; Private; Hampshire Regiment; 1st/4th Battalion; 26; AWM; ASRH; only son of Henry and Ellen Poynter, No. 1 Bow Street, Alton.

RANDALL, WILLIAM DOUGLAS

15 April 1917; Wimereux Communal Cemetery, Pas de Calais, France; 781246; Private; Canadian Infantry; 28th Battalion; 27; AWM; eldest son of Mr and Mrs Frank Randall, No. 21 Victoria Road, Alton, died of wounds received in battle of Vimy Ridge.

RAY, GEORGE

22 September 1914; Portsmouth Naval Memorial, Hampshire; RMA/4579; Sergeant; HMS *Aboukir*; Royal Marine Artillery (RMR/A/0/761); 38; X-AWM; son of George and Mary Ann Ray, Alton, husband of Annie M. Ray, No. 71 Ringwood Road, East Southsea, Portsmouth, Hants, drowned when ship lost.

ROBINSON, WILLIAM HENRY

22 September 1914; Portsmouth Naval Memorial, Hampshire; RMA/2241; Corporal; HMS *Aboukir*; Royal Marine Artillery (RMR/A/0580); AWM; ASRH; landlord of Market Hotel, Alton, drowned when ship lost.

RODWELL, EDWARD JAMES

14 March 1917; Lee (St John the Baptist) Churchyard,
Buckinghamshire; 223557; Driver; Royal Field Artillery; 3rd
Reserve Brigade; 19; X-AWM; son of James and Annie Rodwell,
Overbury Farm, Alton, born at Chesham, died of meningitis.

ROGERS, THOMAS E.

3 May 1915; Menin Gate Memorial, Ypres, Belgium; 3/5191;
Private; Hampshire Regiment; 1st Battalion; AWM; ASRH; left
widow and three children, No. 35 Butts Road, Alton.

ROGERS, WILLIAM EDWARD 'TEDDIE'

5 June 1916; Lyness Royal Naval Cemetery, Orkney, and mentioned
on parents' gravestone in Alton Cemetery; K/24479; Petty Officer
Stoker First Class; HMS *Hampshire*; 19; AWM; ASRH; son of
Mrs R. F. Thompson, No. 8 Lenten Street, Alton, drowned when ship lost.

ROLFE, PERCY

13 July 1915; Helles Memorial, Turkey; PO/11887; Private; Royal
Marines Light Infantry; Portsmouth Battalion, RN Division; 33;
AWM; son of Thomas Rolfe, No. 34 Victoria Road, Alton.

RUFFLE, ALFRED

14 May 1915; Merville Communal Cemetery, France; Z/34; Corporal;
Rifle Brigade; 2nd Battalion; 23; AWM; son of Henry Ruffell (*sic*),
No. 49 Walnut Tree Close, Guildford, worked for Mr E. Low, Alton for eighteen
months before joining up in November 1914, No. 90 High Street, Alton.

RYDER, LEONARD

3 November 1914; Bailleul Communal Cemetery, France; 9422;
Private; Hampshire Regiment; 1st Battalion; AWM; ASRH;
No. 13 Hop Pole Lane, Mount Pleasant Road, Alton.

———— RYDER, WILLIAM STANLEY/SIDNEY GEORGE ————

9 August 1918; Tyne Cot Memorial, Zonnebeke, Belgium; 204851; Private;
Hampshire Regiment; 15th Battalion; Hampshire Yeomanry; 22; AWM;
ASRH; son of William Ryder and Rose (née Hutchins), Orchard Lane,
Alton, husband of Isabella Maggie (née Goddard), No. 16 Lime Tree Cottages,
Rack Close Road, Alton, previously worked for Courage's Brewery.

———— SCARROTT, HENRY ————

8 November 1915; Erquinghem-Lys Churchyard Extension,
France; T/12567; Driver; Army Service Corps; 190th
Company; AWM; died from gas poisoning in France.

———— SIMPSON, RICHARD ————

2 December 1917; Tyne Cot Memorial, Zonnebeke, Belgium; 38597;
Private; Royal Berkshire Regiment; 2nd Battalion; 19; AWM;
son of Mrs Charlotte Enticknap, Wilsom Farm Cottages, Alton.

———— SMALL, GEORGE STEPHEN ————

21 March 1918; Pozieres Memorial, Somme, France; 204176;
Lance Corporal; Essex Regiment; 10th Battalion; 22; AWM; ASRH;
son of James E. and Elizabeth Small, No. 20 Mount Pleasant Road, Alton.

———— SMITH, EDWIN ————

7 May 1917; Vaulx Australian Field Ambulance Cemetery, Pas de Calais,
France; 6585; Private; Australian Infantry; 2nd Battalion; 35; X-AWM;
ASRH; son of Horace and Charlotte Smith, husband of Sarah
Smith, Sydney, Australia, born in Alton, died of wounds.

———— SPENCER, WILLIAM HENRY ————

19 January 1917; Dickebusch New Military Cemetery, Ypres, Belgium;
29122; Machine Gunner (formerly 22426, Hampshire Regiment);
Machine Gun Corps, 123rd Company; AWM; son of William and
Charity Spencer, No. 46 Hereford Road, Southport, Lancashire.

SPREADBURY, E. JOHN

21 August 1918; Abbeville Communal Cemetery Extension, Somme, France; 27406; Private; Canadian Infantry; Central Ontario Regiment; AWM; son of Mrs G. Spreadbury, No. 8 Riverview, Alton, went to Canada aged 18, joined up there, died of wounds in France.

SPREADBURY, THOMAS

14 January 1916; Colne Valley Cemetery, Ypres, Belgium; S/10017; Rifleman; Rifle Brigade (The Prince Consort's Own); 8th Battalion; AWM; born in Basingstoke, lived in Alton, his mother was at Chawton post office in 1916.

STANLEY, JOHN WRIGHT

12 September 1918; Ruyaulcourt Military Cemetery, Pas de Calais, France; 28959; Private; Hampshire Regiment; 2nd/4th Battalion, H Company; AWM (incorrect spelling as Standley); formerly worked at the Gasworks, Alton.

STENNING, FREDERICK

8 November 1918; interred in Alton Cemetery with full military honours; 5267; Private; The Queen's (Royal West Surrey Regiment); 4th Battalion, transfered to (241837) 425th Agricultural Company, Labour Corps; 36; X-AWM, son of Mr and Mrs F. Stenning, Orchard Lane, Alton, husband of Mrs F. Stenning, Victoria Road, Alton, had been in RAMC (1903) and Courage's Brewery, died of pneumonia in Kingston-on-Thames Military Hospital.

STEVENS, ARTHUR CYRIL

13 October 1915; Loos Memorial, Pas de Calais, France; 10537; Corporal; Essex Regiment; 9th Battalion; 22; AWM; son of William and Amy Stevens, No. 5 Sherwood Terrace, Kingsmead, Alton.

STEVENS, WILLIAM WALTER

11 December 1918; Lance Corporal; Hampshire Regiment; 1st/4th Battalion; AWM; died in Maidenhead Hospital, previously worked at Courage's Brewery.

STEWART, EDWARD JOHN

30 November 1917; Moeuvres Communal Cemetery Extension, Nord, France; Second Lieutenant; Machine Gun Corps (Infantry); 140th Company; 24; AWM; eldest son of Mr and Mrs Edward Stewart, Beech, Alton, killed at Bourlon Wood, about 5km west of Cambrai – the scene of fierce and costly fighting during the Battle of Cambrai (20 November–7 December 1917), on the Eggar's Grammar School Roll of Honour.

STOCKER, ARTHUR FREDERICK

2 May 1915; Helles Memorial, Turkey; 7999; Private; Hampshire Regiment; 2nd Battalion; 26; AWM; son of Mrs E. Stocker (née Stacey), Wincoll Villas, Ash Green, Ash, Surrey, died of wounds received at the Dardanelles.

STOCKER, CHARLES JOHN

17 October 1917; Tyne Cot Memorial, Zonnebeke, Belgium; 6227; Lance Corporal; Hampshire Regiment; 14th Battalion; 33; X-AWM; son of the late Charles and Sarah Stocker, husband of Florence Annie Stocker, No. 6 Vicarage Road, Alton.

SUMNER, FREDERICK GEORGE

14 May 1916; Alton Cemetery, Hampshire; b. December 1888; 27; AWM; ASRH; Westleigh, No. 20 Queen's Road, Alton, killed in flying accident.

SUTTABY, JOHN MORTON

26 September 1917; Tyne Cot Memorial, Zonnebeke, Belgium; 5327; Private; Hampshire Regiment; 14th Battalion; 40; AWM; ASRH; son of Mr and Mrs W. Suttaby, No. 39 Queens Road, Alton, brother of Ada Suttaby, Alton.

TARRANT, GEORGE FREDERICK

3 May 1917; Alton Cemetery, Hampshire; T2SR/02683; Driver; Army Service Corps; 560th HT Company (Aldershot); 45; AWM; ASRH; French's Court, High Street, Alton.

THOMAS, A.L.

AWM.

TILBURY, W. (?WILLIAM)

10 october 1916; Grevillers British Cemetery, Pas de Calais, France; 31668; Private; Essex Regiment; 1st Battalion; 28; X-AWM; son of William Tilbury, Falaise, Park Road, Alton, born at Gosport.

TRIMMER, WALTER JAMES

10 October 1917; Tyne Cot Memorial, Zonnebeke, Belgium; 9005; Private; Hampshire Regiment; 2nd Battalion; 23; AWM; son of James Trimmer, Gold Coast, West Africa (1917), worked on Alton Railway.

TRIMMER, WILLIAM EDWARD

6 February 1915; Wimereux Communal Cemetery, Pas de Calais, France; B/2678; Rifleman; Rifle Brigade; 2nd Battalion; 30/31; AWM; son of Robert William and Fanny Trimmer, No. 2 Florence Cottage, Orchard Road, Alton, died of wounds.

TRIMMING, HARRY

10 January 1919; Seale (St Lawrence) Churchyard, Surrey; M2/045734; Private; Royal Army Service Corps, MT; 42; X-AWM; son of Harry Trimming, Alton, husband of Isabella Trimming, Meadow Cottage, Suffield Lane, Puttenham, near Guildford, Surrey.

TUCKER, L.A.

AWM.

TULL, ALBERT WILLIAM HUTTON

26 February 1919; Belgrade Cemetery, Namur, Belgium, also on All Saint's church war memorial, Farringdon, near Alton; T/27093; Lance Corporal; Royal Army Service Corps; 8th Army Auxiliary Horse Transport Company; 28; AWM; son of Mr and Mrs James Tull, husband of Kitty Tull (née Cox), Morland Hall Cottages, Alton, having served in France since 1914 he died of influenza three months after the Armistice was signed.

TULL, ALFRED HENRY

30 November 1917; Cambrai Memorial, Louverval, Nord, France; 243236; Private; Hampshire Regiment; 2nd Battalion; 42; AWM; son of Frederick and Agnes Tull, husband of Mary A. Tull, No. 27 The Butts, Alton.

TULL, WILLIAM

31 August 1916; Basra Memorial, Iraq; 8754; Lance Corporal; Dorsetshire Regiment; 2nd Battalion; 25; AWM; son of Harry and Mary Tull, No. 20 Church Street, Alton, died as POW.

TUNE, HERBERT GEORGE

27 April 1916; Chatham Naval Memorial; J/12786; Able Seaman; HMS *Russell*; 21; AWM.

TURTON, ERNEST

20 September 1915; Azmak Cemetery, Sulva, Turkey; 24729; Private; Manchester Regiment; 11th Battalion; X-AWM; StLRH; husband of Mrs E. Turton, Shalden, Alton.

UNWIN, LANCELOT URQUHART

27 April 1915; Menin Gate Memorial, Ypres, Belgium; Captain; Hampshire Regiment; 1st Battalion; X-AWM; ASRH.

VASS, WILLIAM CHARLES

13 July 1915; Boulogne Eastern Cemetery, Pas de Calais, France; 8439; Private; Somerset Light Infantry; 6th Battalion; 27; X-AWM; son of Thomas and Rosina Vass, husband of R.E.B. Vass, Clifton Lodge, Anstey, Alton, native of Enfield, Middlesex, died of wounds.

VINCE, FREDERICK GEORGE CHARLES

31 May 1916; Portsmouth Naval Memorial; J/20591; Artificer First Class; HMS *Queen Mary*; 19; AWM; son of Ada F. Vince (née Knight), No. 25 Amery Street, Alton, No. 25 Normandy Street, Alton, died in Battle of Jutland.

WALKER, ERNEST GEORGE

26 October 1914; Le Touret Memorial, Pas de Calais, France; 6457; Private; Wiltshire Regiment; 1st Battalion; AWM; New Cottage, Odiham Road, Alton.

WALKER, GEORGE HENRY JAMES

29 March 1918; Namps-au-Val British Cemetery, Somme, France; 33266; Private; Hampshire Regiment; 14th Battalion, D Company; 33; X-AWM; son of George and Louisa Walker, Freemantle, Southampton, husband of Olive Agnes Walker, The Manor House, Alton, died of wounds in France.

WALKER, WILLIAM CHARLES

20 September 1914; La Ferté-Sous-Jouarre Memorial, Seine-et-Marne, France; 7062; Private; Wiltshire Regiment; 1st Battalion; AWM; New Cottage, Odiham Road, Alton.

WARD, J.G.

AWM.

WARNER, DOUGLAS STUART

4 November 1918; Roisel Communal Cemetery Extension, Somme, France; DM2/151518; Private; Army Service Corps; 335 MT Company; b. 10 April 1892; 26; AWM; ASRH; second son of Mr and Mrs W. Warner, No. 47 Queens Road, Alton, joined up on 3 January 1916, m. 26 February 1918.

WARNER, FRANK

3 July 1916; Baghdad (North Gate) War Cemetery, Iraq; 1183; Private; Royal Army Medical Corps, attd 1st/11th Hampshire Regiment; 30; AWM; son of Alfred and Mary Ann Warner, No. 18 Queen's Road, Alton, previously clerk to Mr R. Alward, Farringdon, captured at Kut by Turks and conveyed to Baghdad where he died from disease.

WARREN, CECIL WILLIAM

21 October 1916;Vimy Memorial, Pas de Calais, France; 177515;
Private; Canadian Infantry; 87th Battalion (Quebec); 21; X-AWM;
son of William and Ada Warren, No. 30 Chauntsingers Road, Alton.

WASHINGTON, FREDDIE

31 May 1921; Alton Cemetery, Hampshire; 5485841; Private; Hampshire
Regiment; 2nd Battalion; 19; X-AWM; son of Engineer Washington,
Alton Fire Brigade, one of seven killed by an IRA bomb.

WATTS, GEORGE HENRY

8 February 1916; Tidworth Military Cemetery, Wiltshire; 1696; Private;
Hampshire Yeomanry (Carabineers); 18; AWM; killed at Tidworth.

WEBB, ALBERT EDWARD

26 November 1914; Portsmouth Naval Memorial, Hampshire; 299777
(RFR/PO/B/76574); Petty Officer Stoker; HMS *Bulwark*; 29; AWM; son of
William Webb, Froyle, husband of Winifred Janie Webb, No. 7 Widermouth Villas,
Lower Newport Road, Aldershot, killed when ship blew up off Sheerness.

WEEKS, WILLIAM

31 May 1916; Portsmouth Naval Memorial, Hampshire; 298381; Petty
Officer Stoker; HMS *Invincible*; b. 22 January 1883 at Bentworth; 33;
AWM; son of George and Harriet Weeks, joined the navy aged 18, m. Lily
Florence Binsted at St Lawrence, Alton on 18 February 1905, of No. 60
Normandy Street, Alton, left three children, killed in the Battle of Jutland.

WELLS, FREDERICK,

4 October 1917; Cement House Cemetery, Langemark-Poelkapelle, Belgium;
5317; Company Sergeant Major; Hampshire Regiment; 1st Battalion; 35;
AWM; ASRH; fourth son of Thomas and Elizabeth Wells, Alton, husband
of Louise Wells, No. 17 Bevis Road, Gosport, left three children.

WHITE, B.,

Missing 3 May 1917; Private; Wiltshire Regiment;
X-AWM; StLRH; Turk Street, Alton.

WHITE, CHARLES EDWARD

31 May 1916; Portsmouth Naval Memorial, Hampshire; SS/115423; Stoker
First Class; HMS *Invincible*; 19; AWM; son of Charles Edward and Ellen
Elena White, No. 5 Amery Street, Alton, killed in the Battle of Jutland.

WHITE, HARRY JOHN

28 August 1918; Windmill British Cemetery, Monchy-le-Preux,
Pas de Calais, France; 235007; Private; Somerset Light Infantry;
1st Battalion; 28; AWM; son of Mr and Mrs H.J. White, Nursery
Cottages, Alton, killed by shell on Arras–Cambrai road.

WHITE, HENRY

22 January 1915; Etretat Churchyard Extension, Seine-Maritime,
France; 7803; Private; Hampshire Regiment; 1st Battalion;
X-AWM; No. 6 Sherwood Terrace, Kingsmead, Alton, died of
rheumatic fever, worked for Messrs Crowley & Company.

WHITE, LLOYD ROBERT

1 November 1914; Portsmouth Naval Memorial, Hampshire;
K/9380; Stoker First Class; HMS *Good Hope*; 22; AWM; ASRH;
son of Mrs White, No. 3 Benwells Buildings, Normandy Street,
Alton, killed in the Battle of Coronel, off Chile.

WHITE, PERCY HENRY

26 April 1915; Menin Gate Memorial, Ypres, Belgium; 8940; Private;
Hampshire Regiment; 1st Battalion; 19; AWM; ASRH; son of
Mr R. and Mrs Emily White, No. 29 Turk Street, Alton.

WHITE, PERCY CHARLES GEORGE

AWM.

WHITEAR, WILLIAM ARTHUR

27 September 1918; Queant Communal Cemetery British Extension, Pas de Calais, France; 420804; Private; Canadian Machine Gun Corps; 3rd Battalion; 34; AWM; son of Frederick and Rose Whitear, Mill House, Anstey, Alton.

WHITING, HENRY JAMES, MC

13 June 1916; Alton Cemetery, Hampshire; 31438; Private; Royal Defence Corps, 52 (formerly 209188 Hampshire Regiment); AWM; No. 7 Anstey Terrace, Alton, died of pneumonia at Connaught Hospital, Aldershot, had previously served in India with the Royal Field Artillery.

WICKHAM, WILLIAM GORDON

12 July 1916; Lijssenthoek Military Cemetery, Poperinge, Belgium; A/482; Private; Canadian Infantry; 1st Battalion (West Ontario Regiment); 19; X-AWM; ASRH; son of Frank Gordon and Agnes Mary Wickham, No. 60 Ackender Road, Alton, died of wounds.

WILDEY, RICHARD (DICK)

17 October 1916; Grove Town Cemetery, Meaulte, Somme, France; 71808; Gunner; Royal Field Artillery; 86th Battery, 14th Brigade; 22; AWM; youngest son of George and Mary Jane Frances Wildey of Alton and Medstead, Ackender Cottage, Alton

WILSON, JAMES ANDERSON

6 August 1915; Helles Memorial, Turkey; 3/4937; Company Quartermaster Sergeant; Hampshire Regiment; 2nd Battalion; AWM; formerly cashier at Capital and Counties Bank (merged with Lloyds Bank in 1918), reported missing at Dardanelles, previous service in South African War.

WINDHAM, ARTHUR RUSSELL

30 December 1915; Civilian; b. 1874; 41; X-AWM; included on South Harting war memorial; drowned in sinking of P&O steamer *Persia*, son of Major George Smijth-Windham and Clarissa Elizabeth Russell, m. Brenda Helen Hall on 21 November 1901.

WITHERS, HARRY

4 November 1917; Beersheba War Cemetery, Israel; 200450; Corporal; Royal Sussex Regiment; 1st/4th Battalion; b. October 1890; 27; AWM; ASRH; second son of James and Eliza Withers, No. 14 Ethelmont Terrace, Mount Pleasant Road, Alton, formerly in Church Lads' Brigade, 'a sporting boy'.

WOODS, GEORGE

1 July 1916; Sucrerie Military Cemetery, Colincamps, Somme, France; 15251; Private; Hampshire Regiment; 1st Battalion; 25; AWM; son of John and Mrs Wood, Loes Cottages, Orchard Lane, Alton, formerly worked at Courage's Brewery, brother killed in Boer War.

WORSFOLD, PERCY WILLIAM,

21 January 1916; Basra Memorial, Iraq, also remembered on post office memorial plaque, Royal Mail Sorting Office, Alton, and recorded on Diocesan Bell Ringers' War Memorial, Cathedral Belfry, Winchester; 200042; Sergeant; Hampshire Regiment; 1st/4th Battalion; 37; AWM; son of Edwin and Emily Selina Worsfold, Stonebridge, Shalford, Guildford.

WORTHINGTON, ALFRED GATHORNE

24 July 1915; Basra War Cemetery, Iraq; 1987; Private; Hampshire Regiment; 1st/4th Battalion; 23; AWM; son of Mr H. and Mrs A. Worthington, No. 7 Spitalfields Road, Alton, killed in Persian Gulf.

WRIGHT, ARTHUR

15 September 1916; Aveluy Communal Cemetery Extension, Somme, France; Second Lieutenant; Royal Warwickshire Regiment; 10th Battalion, Machine Gun Corps, attd 33rd Company; AWM; Master at Eggar's School, on Eggar's Grammar School Roll of Honour.

APPENDIX TWO

──────── HOW THE ARMY WAS ORGANISED ────────

Under government legislation of 1907, which followed a review after the South African War, the British Army was reorganised; the Territorial Force was created and included members of the Volunteers and Yeomanry, and the Militia was replaced by the Special Reserve and included men who had not formed part of the Regular Army.

The Hampshire Regiment was composed of a number of battalions, each with a nominal strength of between 800–1,000 men with a lieutenant colonel in command. The 1st and 2nd Battalions consisted of 'Regular' soldiers with one battalion at home and the other overseas, whilst the 3rd was a Reserve Battalion devoted to training. The Territorial Force comprised the 4th, 5th, 6th, 7th and 8th Battalions, these being geographically based at Winchester, Southampton, Portsmouth, Bournemouth and the Isle of Wight respectively, with the 9th being Cyclists and based at Southampton. There were enough men in these units to raise second Territorial Battalions so those based in Winchester and the north of the county, which included the Alton area, formed into the 1st/4th Battalion and the 2nd/4th Battalion. By the end of the war, conscription meant that the number of Service Battalions had reached eighteen.

Each battalion comprised a number of companies of about 160–200 men with a captain in command; platoons contained forty to fifty men with a lieutenant in command, and these were divided into sections of ten to fourteen men under a lance corporal.

For completeness, four regiments comprised a brigade of 3–4,000 men commanded by a brigadier general; three or four brigades comprised a division of 16–18,000 men commanded by a major general and four divisions made up an army commanded by a general.

In the Great War there were three distinct British Armies; the first being the pre-war Regulars and Territorials; the second being Kitchener's Volunteers from

1914–15; whilst the third was formed from men who were conscripted from January 1916.

When the war ended in 1918, British Army casualties, as the result of enemy action and disease, were recorded as 673,375 dead and missing, with another 1,643,469 wounded.

About the Author

TONY CROSS has lived in Alton since 1979 and worked as the curator of the Curtis Museum and Allen Gallery from this date until June 2011. This brought him into daily contact with the town, its people and their past, providing him with a unique insight into the richness of Alton's history. Tony currently works at Amery Hill School as well as for the Open University and enjoys photography, giving talks on a variety of topics, continuing his research into the men whose names are on the town's war memorial and walking the family dog.

Tony is associated with a number of books on Alton and the surrounding area; has contributed to *Alton Papers*, an annual local history journal produced by the Friends of the Curtis Museum and Allen Gallery; and has written numerous articles on a variety of historical and geological topics for newspapers, magazines and journals. He is an active member of the Alton Decorative and Fine Arts Society and has edited their newsletter since 2005.

BIBLIOGRAPHY

PRIMARY SOURCES

Most of the details contained here came from primary material. Much of the information on families came from census returns, births, marriage and death records, and newspapers – especially the *Hampshire Herald & Alton Gazette* which is available on microfilm at Alton Library. Details of an individual's military service have come from a variety of sources, including Medal Roll Cards, *Soldiers Died in the Great War* and *Officers Died in the Great War* databases, the archives of the Hampshire Regimental Museum, information collated by the Commonwealth War Graves Commission and material contained in the collections of the Hampshire Record Office. The archives of Alton Abbey were most useful with regard to the German sailors at the start of the war and the Brothers who chose to serve in the forces.

Family members of some of those who were involved in the Great War provided relevant information including photographs. The Royal Naval Museum, Portsmouth, was a splendid source of illustrations of naval vessels. The collections of the Hampshire Cultural Trust, previously Hampshire County Council Museums Service, were a very good source of material and illustrations.

An exercise book containing the Roll of Honour (a list of all the men from Alton who served during the Great War) compiled by Revd C.R. Stebbing Elvin of St Lawrence church, Alton, was a vital source and it came to light during the project. The Rolls of Honour produced by Courage & Co., Crowley & Co., St Lawrence church, All Saints' church, the Post Office and Eggar's Grammar School also provided useful details.

—————————— SECONDARY SOURCES ——————————

Anon., *2/4 Battalion Hampshire Regiment 1914–1919* (compiled by officers and printed by the regiment, 1919).

Atkinson, C.T., *The Royal Hampshire Regiment, 1914–1918*, Vol. 2 (Glasgow: The University Press, 1952).

Brice, M., *Hampshire in the Great War*, edited by T. Cross and N. Gosling (a joint publication by Hampshire Record Office and Hampshire County Museums Service, 1985).

Clark, C., *The Sleepwalkers: How Europe Went to War in 1914* (Penguin Press, 2013).

Coombes, R.E.B., *Before Endeavours Fade – A Guide to the Battlefields of the First World War* (After the Battle, 2006, twelfth edition).

Corbett, Sir Julian S., *Naval Operations* (Longmans, Green & Co., 1923).

Cox, J.H., *An Ordinary Working Man's Life Story* (Alton, 1967).

Cross, T., 'Lest We Forget – The Story of Alton's War Memorial' in *Alton Papers 2* (Friends of the Curtis Museum and Allen Gallery, 1998).

Crowley, P., *Kut 1916 – Courage and Failure in Iraq* (Stroud: The History Press, 2009).

Ferguson, N., *The Pity of War 1914–1918* (Penguin Press, 1998).

Hart, P., *Gallipoli* (Profile Books, 2011).

Hart, P., *The Great War* (Profile Books, 2013).

Hegarty, S. and F. O'Toole, *The Irish Times Book of the 1916 Rising* (Gill & Macmillan, 2006).

Longworth, P., *The Unending Vigil – The History of the Commonwealth War Graves Commission* (Leo Cooper, 1967. Revised and updated in 1985, reprinted in 2003).

Stevenson, D., *With Our Backs to the Wall – Victory and Defeat in 1918* (Allen Lane, 2011).

Storey, N.R., and M. Housego, *Women in the First World War* (Shire Publications, 2010).

—————————— WEBSITES ——————————

Alton War Memorial: www3.hants.gov.uk/curtis-museum/alton-history/lest-we-forget.htm

Battle of Jutland: www.battle-of-jutland.com

Commonwealth War Graves Commission: www.cwgc.org

First World War: www.firstworldwar.com

Gallipoli: www.gallipoli-association.org

King's African Rifles Association: www.kingsafricanriflesassociation.co.uk

Soldiers' Wills: www.probatesearch.service.gov.uk

Naval History: www.naval-history.net/index.htm

Royal Engineers Light Railway Companies: www.1914-1918.net/lightrail.htm

The Great War: www.greatwar.co.uk

The Long, Long Trail: www.1914-1918.net/army.htm

U-Boat Net: www.uboat.net/index.html

Western Front Association: www.westernfrontassociation.com

INDEX